LOVE SAYS

SAMANTHA GILLION

LOVE SAYS

Discover and Believe The Love God Has For You

Love Says
First Edition, First Impression 2021
ISBN: 978-1-77630-681-7

Published by:
Inspired Publishing
PO Box 82058 | Southdale | 2135
Johannesburg , South Africa
Email: info@inspiredpublishing.co.za
www.inspiredpublishing.co.za

TABLE OF CONTENTS

Dedication

RJ and Aimee, you gave me the title I am proudest of the most and the one that has stretched me to become more myself than any other.

You are made for signs, wonders and miracles by God who is Love, you belong to Him, and wherever this life may lead you, I want you to always walk in the confidence that God Almighty chose you to be His own. The only opinion in this world that matters is what God thinks of you. Love Him with all your heart and live boldly for His glory.

I see your eyes on me, and so I dare to live in my purpose so you can do the same. I will never be able to put into words how much I love you, but I will spend my whole life showing you the best I know how.

My prayers for you are the greatest gift I have to give you, so I will give them to you multiple times a day.

I pray that out of His glorious riches, He may strengthen you with power through His Spirit in your inner being so that Christ may dwell in your hearts through faith. And I pray that you, being rooted and established in love, may have power, together with all the Lord's holy people, to grasp how wide and long and high and deep is the love of Christ and to know this love that surpasses knowledge that you may be filled to the measure of all the fullness of God. Now to Him who is able to do immeasurably more than all we ask or imagine, according to His power that is at work within us, to Him be glory in the church and in Christ Jesus throughout all generations, forever and ever! Amen.

You bring the greatest joy to your dad and me; thank you for being the most amazing son and daughter any parents could have.
You will forever be my heart and my babies.

Thank You

My sweet Jesus:
I live to see you one day! Thank you for giving me everything I need to help me get to where you are and spend an eternity with you! I love you, Lord!

My loving husband, Ranvor John Gillion
I prayed for you since I was 14 years old, not knowing your name but Jesus knew. You are my Ephesians 3:20 answered prayer; you have exceeded all of my hearts expectations. With you, I didn't find perfection. I found love, happiness, joy, belonging, encouragement and my forever home.

I honour you for always allowing me to dream, for believing I can, when I'm still swimming in my rivers of doubt, for being the most amazing dad and always putting our family first. I bless the day you were born Ranvor; you are forever my person.

I pray the favour of God over your life. I pray that the eyes of your heart may be enlightened so that you may know the hope to which He has called you, the riches of His glorious inheritance in His holy people, and His incomparably great power for us who believe. Thank you for loving me so well. I love you forever, my forever.

My darling mommy, Maria Daniels
I am eternally grateful to God that He chose you to be my mother, my best friend and my spiritual mother too. Life has not always been easy for you, but you have given us the greatest gift any child could need; you chose Jesus, and you chose a life of faith. Mommy, you are everything I hope to become, and I cannot put into words how proud I am to be your daughter.

I pray that you will continue to see the goodness of the Lord in the land of the living, that God will make you into a great nation, and bless you and make your name great and that you will be a blessing to all you encounter. Thank you, Mommy, for choosing life, so we can have life. I love you.

To my amazing family
Thank you for always supporting me, loving me, and believing in my dreams. My prayer for all of you is that you will know and accept the great love of Jesus Christ, that you may live in the abundance of His love and blessings.

CHAPTER 1

Princess, let's talk

The greatest truth that I ever discovered in my life is that I am loved. The irony in this discovery was the fact that I was never not loved. You see, being loved and knowing that you are loved are two very different things.

Because the truth is that all of us have always been loved, we were created in love, by love and for love.

I know that this might sound strange if you were abandoned by a mother, a father or both, or if you grew up in a very abusive home or lived in severe poverty or were born with a disability, whatever your circumstances were that causes you not to believe this truth. As strange as it sounds, it remains the truth and nothing, we or anybody else can

do can ever change this.
Because we were created by God the creator of the universe, and He says, before I formed you in the womb I knew you … (Jeremiah 1:5).
The word of God has the final authority over everything, and this is what He says about you!

Psalm 139:13-18
For you created my inmost being;
you knit me together in my mother's womb.
I praise you because I am fearfully and wonderfully made;
your works are wonderful,
I know that full well.
My frame was not hidden from you
when I was made in the secret place.
When I was woven together in the depths of the earth,
your eyes saw my unformed body.
All the days ordained for me were written in your book
before one of them came to be.
How precious to me are your thoughts, O God!
How vast is the sum of them!
Were I to count them,
they would outnumber the grains of sand.
When I awake, I am still with you.

Being born in love has nothing to do with who our mother and father is but has everything to do with who God Almighty created us is. We live in a fallen world where we have all fallen short of the glory of God. The human heart will fail us; no one is ever going to be perfect, and just because the person that you expect should show you love does not, it does not mean you are not loved.

But if the enemy can convince you that you are not loved, not wanted, that your existence is a mistake and that how you got to be, matters more than why you got to be, he will succeed in keeping you from living a glorified life for Christ.

We were created by God who is Love, for God who is Love and in the image of God who is Love. Our existence was never a surprise to God. God loves you so much. We know this because the word of God says in *John 3:16 - For God so loved the world, that He gave His only begotten Son, that whosoever believeth on him should not perish, but have eternal life.*

I am sure (sincerely hopeful) that if you are reading this book, you might have heard about or read this Scripture at some point in your life. Now read it again, memorise it, write it on the tables of your heart because it is the foundation, the heart of the gospel of Jesus Christ and the depth of just how much God loves you.

In His pursuit of us, God gave us what He has always valued most, His Son. Jesus suffered greatly on the cross so that we would not have to. Every time I think of the magnitude of that act of love, I cannot fathom how the God of the universe could love me that much, and yet He does, and at the end of the day, that is the only truth that matters.

Father To The Fatherless

Let me start by telling you about our Father the Hero.

Psalm 68:5
A father to the fatherless, a defender of widows, is God in his holy dwelling

Born to a single mother who was just 20 years old in the 1980s. My grandparents raised me until my granny died when I was only six years old. I would live between my grandfather and some other family members until the age of 10 after which I would go and live with my mom, dad (technically speaking, he was my stepdad, but we never did refer to him as that) and my brother.

The truth is that even though I did not know who my biological father was, I always had some form of a father figure in my life. My grandfather was a hard and strict man, but he loved God, and he loved me. My dad had his own struggles in life; he was abusive towards my mother, which was very hard to see. The one thing that I do remember is that with all his struggles, I do believe he loved me the best way he knew how. However, the enemy will use whatever he can to cause us to look for what we perceive we lack and overlook what we have.

Because my grandparents were born-again Christians, I knew of God from a very early age. The fondest memory I have of my grandmother is that she taught me Psalm 23, and I was able to recite it off by heart at the age of six. I did not really understand the truth of that passage then, but it would become a portion of Scripture that would help me through the difficult seasons of my life.

When I think of my life story and the very beginning of my relationship with the Lord Jesus, I always think of the song by Cece Winans :

"Mercy said no"
I was just a child, when I felt the Savior leading
I was drawn to what I could not understand
And for the cause of Christ, I have spent my days believing

That what He'd have me be, who I am.

I remember the night I accepted Christ as my saviour, and God became my Father. I was 13 years old, attending youth at our local church. I remember the altar call, the stirring in my heart, walking to the front and praying the salvation prayer.

Having grown up never knowing who my biological father was and not fully comprehending what aftereffects it would have on my life at the time, that encounter shaped the rest of my life in a significant way. Years after accepting Christ into my heart, and the prayer that changed everything for me, I would get a complete revelation of what accepting God as a father really did for me that night.

As I share my heart and what the Holy Spirit is leading me to write, my prayer is that in the pages of this book, you will not only discover the great love of God our Father, the greatest love you will ever know, but that you may also accept the love of the Father and live in the fullness of what it all means for you.

Ephesians 3:14-19

For this reason I kneel before the Father, from whom every family in heaven and on earth derives its name. I pray that out of his glorious riches he may strengthen you with power through his Spirit in your inner being, so that Christ may dwell in your hearts through faith. And I pray that you, being rooted and established in love, may have power, together with all the Lord's holy people, to grasp how wide and long and high and deep is the love of Christ, and to know this love that surpasses knowledge—that you may be filled to the measure of all the fullness of God.

CHAPTER 2

This is Love

1 John 4:10
This is love: not that we loved God, but that he loved us and sent his Son as an atoning sacrifice for our sins.

At some point in our lives, most of us would have loved someone who did not love us back. This is one of the most painful things to go through, and you might even try to win over that person for a while, but at some point, you would give up and move on; that is the difference between us humans and God. He never gives up on us.

He is relentless in pursuing us; the greatest love story written will always be this one that God loved us so much that He sent His only Son Jesus Christ to die for us. *But God demonstrated His own love for us in this: that while we were still sinners, Christ died for us. (Romans 5:8).* Because this love was never based on anything that we did or will do. We can rest assured that it cannot change because of anything we did or will do, the Bible says: *No, in all these things we are more than conquerors through him who loved us.* For I am convinced that neither death nor life, neither angels nor demons, neither the present nor the future, nor any powers, neither height nor depth, nor anything else in all creation, will be able to separate us from the love of God that is in Christ Jesus our Lord *(Romans 8:37-39).*

God's Love Is The Standard

We can never expect any human, no matter how great their faith or how well they live and ever to love us the way God loves us; it just will not happen, as humans we are flawed, and we will fail each other's expectations in some way at some point.

But this is what I mean when I say that God's love should be the standard. The Bible teaches us that: All Scripture is God-breathed and is useful for teaching ... (2 Timothy 3:16).

And true to His word, God teaches us about what love should look like. Even though many of the definitions given about love refer to it being a feeling or an emotion, the Bible teaches us differently.
We find that in the Bible, love is mostly an action word. In the greatest, most known passage of Scripture about love, used at the most wedding as the foundation that we set out to live by, Paul says this about what love is:

1 Corinthians 13:4-7
Love is patient, love is kind. It does not envy, it does not boast, it is not proud. It does not dishonor others, it is not self-seeking, it is not easily angered, it keeps no record of wrongs. Love does not delight in evil but rejoices with the truth. It always protects, always trusts, always hopes, always perseveres.

As a woman, I find our desire to be loved far exceeds any other desires we might have. In fact, almost every action we take can somehow be linked back to wanting to be loved. Always working towards being beautiful, smart, and accomplished, hoping that somehow this will make us worthy of finding love.

Ephesians 5:22-28

Wives, submit yourselves to your own husbands as you do to the Lord. For the husband is the head of the wife as Christ is the head of the church, his body, of which he is the Savior. Now as the church submits to Christ, so also wives should submit to their husbands in everything.
Husbands, love your wives, just as Christ loved the church and gave himself up for her to make her holy, cleansing her by the washing with water through the word, and to present her to himself as a radiant church, without stain or wrinkle or any other blemish, but holy and blameless. In this same way, husbands ought to love their wives as their own bodies. He who loves his wife loves himself.

God created us this way, knit us together in this specific way, and this is the very reason that the enemy will be on the frontline of attacking our desire to be loved. I believe with all my heart that when we discover and truly live like women who are completely loved, we become powerful beyond measure, and we are able to change the world. The enemy knows that we hold that power within us, and as much as we can change the world for good, if we believe the lie about love, the one that the devil has deceived so many with, over the centuries, we can change the world for the worst.

What I see happen in the world today is that this deep desire to be loved has caused us as women to settle for anything that resembles what we consider to be love. Do not be deceived in this way any longer. The God who says I love you has given you His Word, and He teaches us what love should look like.

We need to get to a place where we know what the word of God says and know that anything contrary to the word is lies from the enemy. The Psalmist says that the Lord guides us along the right paths for His name's sake (Psalm 23:3). We need to measure the love we are looking for against the standard set out by Paul; we need to be bold in our pursuit and not compromise or apologise for seeking this kind of love. Are you in a relationship right now where you know with a sure conviction you should not be in because you are not receiving love according to what God's word says it should look like?

I want you to ask yourself: Is he patient with me? Is He kind to me? Is he jealous of me or jealous over me? (Yes, both are wrong, stop convincing yourself that him being jealous over you is love). Is he boastful or proud? Is he rude to me? Does he always demand his own way? Is he consistently irritable towards me? Does he always remind me of all the things that I did wrong? Does he stand up for injustice and walk in truth? Is he someone that stands by me and endures the good and the tough circumstances?

Always keep in mind that no one is perfect and will live up to all this 100%. But a Godly man that truly lives for God will seek to grow to love you like this; if you do not yet see that fruit, you should be able to identify the seed. So stop settling for just anything, I will go as far as to say stop settling for a good man, but seek God and wait for a Godly man, someone you know has a love for Christ and fully walks in the truth of the word of God. He will live with the Holy Spirit inside him who will lead him in all truth in life and love.

God's love should not only be the standard that you seek but also that standard to which you hold yourself in your pursuit to love well. If you desire a man after God's own heart, seek to be a woman after God's own heart. I challenge you to ask yourself the same question directed at yourself. Am I patient? Am I kind? Am I jealous of or over people? Am I boastful or proud? Am I rude? Do I always demand my own way? Am I consistently irritable towards people? Do I always remind people of the wrong they did to me? Do I stand up for injustice and walk in truth? Am I someone who stands by people and endures the good and the tough circumstances? I encourage you to seek a truth-teller in your life and seek out feedback from that person on the above. Remember to remain in Jesus, remain in His love. Then you will know how to love each other well.

John 15: 9-12

As the Father has loved me, so have I loved you. Now remain in my love. If you keep my commands, you will remain in my love, just as I have kept my Father's commands and remain in his love. I have told you this so that my joy may be in you and that your joy may be complete. My command is this: Love each other as I have loved you.

A King And A Father

I remember an interview that Prince Harry and his wife Meghan Markle, the Duchess of Sussex, had with Oprah Winfrey; there was one incident that Meghan spoke of her first time meeting the Queen. It was meant to be a spur of the moment meeting as they were on their way to lunch when Harry mentioned it and asked her if she knew how to curtsy. Meghan relayed that she was taken aback and responded with, but she is your grandmother, and Harry responded for a matter of fact, yes, but she is also the queen.

Growing up, I remember being taught to see God as more of a master, Lord, Ruler and King; I do not remember the older generation teaching us about God being a soft, kind and loving father. So I realised that if God is my King, I ought to have respect and reverence, and it should show in the way I walked, talked, dressed, basically the way I lived when in His presence and when I represented Him in any capacity.

As I began to walk closer with God, I realised that He is also my Father, and He wants me to relate to Him as a loving Father. Much like Meghan, I was confused as to where the one ends and the other starts.
One of many Scriptures that show us that God wants to relate to us as our spiritual Father is in The Lord's Prayer (Matthew 6:9). Jesus teaches us to relate to God as "Our Father in heaven." In other words, God is our good and flawless spiritual Father, and we are to relate to Him as such too.

As I developed a relationship with God and saw more into the father heart of God, it has healed many wounds in my own soul, specifically the emptiness of not having known my own earthly father. I have seen the side of God in the Scriptures that have made me fall in love with Him and accept the gift of being His daughter. Slowly I began to understand that God wants us to relate to Him as both our Father and our King at the same time.

Yet, we need to always seek the Holy Spirit in bringing this to our remembrance. The fact that God is a Father to us does not cancel out that He is also King. In God, we have a beautiful mixture of both. We need to find that balance in prayer and reading God's word because if we focus so deeply on the father heart of God, we run the risk of becoming too relaxed in your pursuit of obedience and may lose some of the weight of God's holiness. At the same time, we should not see God as only King, or we become legalistic and self-righteous in our walk with God. We lose the hope that is found in His grace and the gift that was given to us at the cross.

The most beautiful revelation in this all is that because God is both our Father and our King, it makes us both his daughter and a princess. Just like our lives change, we are no longer just mere citizens of this earth. We cannot just be the same; we represent our Father the King from now until the day of Christ return.
God, our Father, says that we are blessed, we are called, we are chosen, and we are adopted into sonship through Jesus Christ.

Ephesians 1:2-7
Grace and peace to you from God our Father and the Lord Jesus Christ. Praise be to the God and Father of our Lord Jesus Christ, who has blessed us in the heavenly realms with every spiritual blessing in Christ. For he chose us in him before the creation of the world to be holy and blameless in his sight. In love he predestined us for adoption to sonship through Jesus Christ, in accordance with his pleasure and will–to the praise of his glorious grace, which he has freely given us in the One he loves. In him we have redemption through his blood, the forgiveness of sins, in accordance with the riches of God's grace.

God the King requires us to pursue righteousness, godliness, faith, love, endurance, and gentleness, to fight the good fight and live with an eternal perspective.

1 Timothy 6:11-16
But you, man of God, flee from all this, and pursue righteousness, godliness, faith, love, endurance and gentleness. Fight the good fight of the faith. Take hold of the eternal life to which you were called when you made your good confession in the presence of many witnesses. In the sight of God, who gives life to everything, and of Christ Jesus, who while testifying before Pontius Pilate made the good confession, I charge you to keep this command without spot or blame until the appearing of our Lord Jesus Christ, which God will bring about in his own time–God, the blessed and only Ruler, the King of kings and Lord of lords, who alone is immortal and who lives in unapproachable light, whom no one has seen or can see. To him be honor and might forever. Amen

In the Lord's Prayer: " Hallowed be Thy name" means we treat God as Holy, He is our King. We do this by sharing the truth of who He is with others and living a life of obedience, surrender and honour to Him.

When we find the revelation of all that God is to us, this will allow us to speak to God differently, listen, worship, and respond to Him differently. The way we read Scriptures will shift, and the way we value God, others, and ourselves will be different. How we relate to God as Father and King affects how we see, speak, and ultimately live.

I pray that God will grant you the gracious gift of knowing Him as a loving father, walking beside Him, His hand in yours, his daughter. Also, serving Him with honour and wonder and taking your rightful place as her royal highness as the princess of heaven.

CHAPTER 3

LOVE SAYS: *You are Forgiven*

Ephesians 1:7
In him we have redemption through his blood,
the forgiveness of sins, in accordance with the riches of God's grace.

For me accepting Christ into my heart at a very young age, it did not seem that I had a lot to ask forgiveness for. As the years went by, I often thought that my salvation story was not powerful enough to share with anyone. Then I came to the realisation that this is the enemy trying to deceive me. We need to be aware of his tactics.

Deception: My Sin Is Too Great; God Cannot Forgive Me

The first one is the most common and maybe most obvious one, he will tell you that the sin you committed was too bad for God ever to forgive you. If you have ever felt the hopelessness and regret upon discovering how bad your sin really was if you are saying: 'if you only knew the things I have done, how can God forgive me?"

I want you to know that you are not alone in feeling that way. We read of many in the Bible who were crushed by the weight of their sin. The Apostle Paul being the most relatable person when it comes to this, he calls himself "the worst of sinners". Here is a trustworthy saying that deserves full acceptance: Christ Jesus came into the world to save sinners—of whom I am the worst (1 Timothy 1:15).

This is a man whose main mission in life was to destroy the church and put both men and women in prison, which he did. He was hardcore when it came to sin, this was a man who was feared by believers in those days, and this is also the same man that God called His chosen one.

Act 8:3
But Saul began to destroy the church. Going from house to house, he dragged off both men and women and put them in prison.

Acts 9:13-16
"Lord," Ananias answered, "I have heard many reports about this man and all the harm he has done to your holy people in Jerusalem. And he has come here with authority from the chief priests to arrest all who call on your name." But the Lord said to Ananias, "Go! This man is my chosen instrument to proclaim my name to the Gentiles and their kings and to the people of Israel. I will show him how much he must suffer for my name.

Saul, who would become the great Apostle Paul, was the least likely person you would ever imagine to be called by God Almighty. This is if we measured by human standards. But the good news about the gospel of Jesus, the power of the blood shed on the cross, and the resurrection of Jesus is why we do not have to stay bound to who we have been or even who we are in this moment. A doctor does not study for years to become a doctor to treat healthy people; there would be no point in doing that. In the same way, there would be no need for Jesus to die if sin did not enter the world. Unfortunately, it did, and He did die, and He has risen, and because of the cross, we have redemption and the forgiveness of sin.

The most important decision we will ever make is choosing to believe the truth, for God so loved the world that he gave His only begotten Son, that whoever believes in Him shall not perish, but have eternal life (John 3:16).
Christ died for all the world to be saved. Do not allow the enemy to convince you that you do not deserve this redemption.

Deception: My Sin Is Not That Bad; I Do Not Need Forgiveness

The second way might be more difficult to see; at first sight, the enemy will convince you that the sin you feel is either not really sin or just too small to validate you having to ask for God's forgiveness. The Bible says: *"if we say we have no sin, we deceive ourselves, and the truth is not in us" (1 John 1:8).*

What I learned in discovering this is that if we allow the enemy to deceive us in this way, both of those lies will lead us into eternal condemnation, and we will burn in the lake of fire. To God, sin is sin; repentance will lead you to eternal life with Him.

Therefore we need to believe that Jesus loved us so completely that He sacrificed himself and bore the sin of the world as His own. There is no sin that His death did not already pay for. *God made him who had no sin to be sin for us, so that in him we might become the righteousness of God" (2 Corinthians 5:21).*

The love that says I will forgive you does apply to all of us; without the belief in that truth and without repentance, we will fall prey to the devil, who is the ultimate deceiver.

Always remember these two things. One, no sin is too big or bad that God cannot forgive you and two, no sin is too small or insignificant that it does not require the forgiveness of God. The Bible says, *for all have sinned and fall short of the glory of God (Romans 3:23).*

Many times, I thought of my story; I had grown up in a Christian home, with grandparents that brought me the foundation of the Gospel. God called my name at a young age, and for me, the beauty of my salvation story is the amazing grace that I was able to find Christ at such a young age. I do not know what the path might have led to had I not said yes to God.

As you continue to read this book, I will tell of the some of the consequences the sin of disobedience has caused me, and sometimes I wonder what might have happened had I not been obedient to the call from God that night; I do know that obedience to the call of salvation, repentance of my sin and believing that Christ died for me saved my life.

Now I know that my salvation story is not about how big or small my sin was but how great the God of Heaven and earth is that He would send His son to die for my sin. So when God called my name that night in a church in Gauteng during a small youth service, the redemptive power that washed me clean was the same power that met Paul on the road to Damascus.

Deception: I Do Not Need To Forgive To Be Forgiven

Matthew 6:14-15
For if you forgive other people when they sin against you, your heavenly Father will also forgive you. But if you do not forgive others their sins, your Father will not forgive your sins.

When the words in this passage first reached the depth of my heart, I was so shaken by the magnitude of what the consequences are for a person with an unforgiving heart. It is eternal condemnation! Yes, you read it right for those who cannot forgive; there can be no forgiveness of their sins.

The Unmerciful Servant

Matthew 18:21-35
Then Peter came to Jesus and asked, "Lord, how many times shall I forgive my brother or sister who sins against me? Up to seven times? Jesus answered, "I tell you, not seven times, but seventy-seven times "Therefore, the kingdom of heaven is like a king who wanted to settle accounts with his servants. As he began the settlement, a man who owed him ten thousand bags of gold was brought to him. Since he was not able to pay, the master ordered that he and his wife and his children and all that he had be sold to repay the debt. "At this the servant fell on his knees before him. 'Be patient with me,' he begged, 'and I will pay back everything.' The servant's master took pity on him, cancelled the debt and let him go. "But when that servant went out, he found one of his fellow servants who owed him a hundred silver coins. He grabbed him and began to choke him. 'Pay back what you owe me!' he demanded. "His fellow servant fell to his knees and begged him, 'Be patient with me, and I will pay it back.'" But he refused. Instead, he went off and had the man thrown into prison until he could pay the debt. When the other servants saw what had happened, they were outraged and went and told their master everything that had happened. "Then the master called the servant in. 'You wicked servant,' he said, 'I cancelled all that debt of yours because you begged me to. Shouldn't you have had mercy on your fellow servant just as I had on you?' In anger his master handed him over to the jailers to be tortured, until he should pay back all he owed. "This is how my heavenly Father will treat each of you unless you forgive your brother or sister from your heart."

The revelation of this parable might seem harsh to many, especially if you are dealing with extreme hurt. It might seem unfair that God would ask this of you. The truth is that it is not harsh or unfair at all. It is an amazing affirmation of the great love of Christ.

I want you to think about how, what that person had done to you affected you, and how it made you feel. I know it might be hard, but this is what I want you to imagine, not feeling that feeling anymore. Imagine not being angry, or bitter, or broken. Do you know that that is what you forgiving them will do for you? It will bring you the freedom that you have been longing for. You see, God promises us life in abundance. We cannot receive and enjoy all that God has for us if we have no forgiveness in our hearts.

The good news is that you do not have to do it by yourself; God gave us the Holy Spirit who will give us the strength to do what seems impossible. I have learned that forgiveness is just as much about me as it is about the person I am forgiving.

When we think about it, Jesus was sinless, pure, and perfect, but he came so that we did not have to pay the price that was required to be paid.
Forgiveness of sins is the core of our salvation story because, without it, there is no salvation; if God had not sent Jesus to die for our sins, we would always fall short. The Bible places so much importance on the forgiveness of sins that God says in His word that if we do not forgive other people, he cannot forgive us. If we are walking around with unforgiveness in our hearts, then God cannot forgive us; that is how serious God is about forgiveness of sins.

God would not be a God of pure unconditional love if He would put something in place where He is saying to us that if we cannot forgive, he cannot forgive us, knowing full well that our sins could stretch so far that in any human capacity if we did do to each other some of the things we do against God we will never be able to forgive each other. But because God is so gracious towards us, he is able to forgive us everything and anything he requires of us to be able to forgive each other. That is, after all, the core of what God's love is. Love forgives, and if we love, we need to forgive others.

James 5:16

Therefore, confess your sins to one another and pray for one another, that you may be healed. The prayer of a righteous person is powerful and effective.

Growing up, I loved the idea of love; I think that what drew me in is this idea that God loved me. Even though, as a young teenage girl, I did not truly understand what that would look like, I knew enough to know that when someone loved you, it meant something good. However, the older I got, I realised that what the Bible said about love was not really the reality of the love people loved out in the world.

I saw how my dad would abuse my mom when he was drunk and apologised after, and my mom would always stay. She stayed for over 20 years. I did not realise how this affected my thoughts on what real love looked like until many years later. My dad was never ever mean to any of us kids. In fact, he treated us better than I saw some of my friends own fathers treat them. It was his treatment of my mother that was the problem.

A few years into being married and having had my first child, I was sitting in my house, and I remember looking around and seeing my home and the life God gave me with a husband who loved me well. I felt sadness that instantly turned into anger, which well up in me. I never realised that I had held onto some things that were holding me back from truly enjoying the goodness of God in the season I was in.

I was angry at my dad for treating my mom so badly, I was angry that she missed out on being loved the way any woman deserves, but I realised that I was also angry at my mother for staying as long as she did. I felt in my heart that had she left, she might have found someone who would have really loved her.

I cried that day because the revelation in my heart that I was carrying this shocked me because that meant I had unforgiveness towards my mom and dad. I did not like that, because I was aware of what that meant. So I asked

God what I was to do now.

The following Sunday, I went to church, and I remember the pastor doing an altar call. He was calling on someone who had bitterness towards a relationship where someone they loved had hurt them, and they were unable to forgive. I remember thinking he was talking about a romantic relationship and knew this was not for me. As soon as the thought came up in my mind, he said these exact words "it can be any relationship, maybe a parent-child relationship", and I knew God was calling me to repentance for something I didn't even know I was holding onto for so long.

At this point in my life, I was a believer for long enough to know that when God touches something that He needs to heal, it is because it is the thing that the enemy will want to use against me in the future. I got up for prayer and asked God to help me to forgive and give me the answers I needed.

A few weeks later, we had a woman's camp that was hosted by my mother. On the Saturday of the camp, during the morning session, God led my mother to share her testimony with the woman; I never told her what had happened a few weeks prior. In her testimony, she shared why she had stayed so long. I was so in awe of what God was doing because I finally got it, and I knew that God wanted this part of my heart to be healed even though for many years, I did not know it needed healing. He healed me at the age of 31, and I felt the freedom to truly enjoy and be thankful for a husband that loved me so well.

Sometimes we cover up our hurts and convince ourselves that we have overcome, but if true forgiveness does not happen, we will find ourselves in a place of bitterness and resentment when we least expect it.

The emotions triggered that day on the couch might have caught me off guard, but it did not catch God off guard; He sees into the deepest parts of our hearts.

He is the love that forgives, but it will require us to come to the cross with our sins, our own unforgiveness and our disappointments. I have seen many times how bitterness can destroy lives. It took me to admit that I was angry because I was trying to get to a place where I realised that my heart needed healing from what unforgiveness has caused over the years.

God could have let me be because, by this time, I had a wonderful husband, a son, and a beautiful home. My mother was settled in a beautiful ministry and living in her own home. It did not make sense to go and dig up the past, right? But you see, God sees where we cannot see, and He knows that if we have not completely forgiven, we cannot be completely healed from our brokenness, and we cannot receive His forgiveness, and the enemy has a hold on us.

I know that your hurt and your brokenness might be so much bigger and worse than I could ever imagine; maybe you saying what has been done to me is just too horrible, I will never be able to forgive, but I want you to know that the God who is love, is saying to you that the He is your ever-present help in time of need. Ask God to help you to forgive. Jesus gives us the perfect example, while He was on the cross, he cried out to God, *"Father, forgive them for they know not what they are doing" (Luke 23:34).*

God's forgiveness is for you, for me and for those people that need our forgiveness too.

The one thing that the enemy will consistently try to convince you God's love cannot do is forgive you, and He will use your unforgiveness towards someone else to keep you in a place of bondage and keep you from being in perfect peace with God. You need to break free from that; you need to start with believing that.

God's love is many things, as you will see as you continue to read this book. But the most important part is knowing that it is unconditional and that that love forgives you for all your sins that have separated you from Him; Adam and Eve caused that separation right in the beginning. As the great Father that He is and with the great love, He has for us, God knows the importance of forgiveness. Without it, there will forever be a separation between the person we cannot forgive and us, which will ultimately lead to continued separation between God and us.

Forgiveness is God's gift to us to live well, live abundantly in the world. His word says that He came that we might have life and have it in abundance. (John 10:10)

Matthew 18:21-22

Then Peter came to Jesus and asked, "Lord, how many times shall I forgive my brother or sister who sins against me? Up to seven times?" Jesus answered, "I tell you, not seven times, but seventy-seven times.

Exodus 34:7

maintaining love to thousands, and forgiving wickedness, rebellion and sin. Yet he does not leave the guilty unpunished; he punishes the children and their children for the sin of the parents to the third and fourth generation.

So many people have been deceived into thinking that the finished work of Jesus guarantees us an automatic seat in the heavenly realms. Yes, Jesus paid the ultimate price; He won the victory! But we still need to accept the gift of salvation and accept Christ as our personal Lord and Saviour.
How do you give your life to Jesus?

Confess Your Sins

1 John 1:9 If we confess our sins, he is faithful and just and will forgive us our sins and purify us from all unrighteousness.

Remember, you are not unique in being a sinner, for all have sinned, but God is not only able to forgive you but also to cleanse you completely if you boldly come to Him and confess your sins.

Turn Away From Your Sin

Acts 3:19 Repent, then, and turn to God, so that your sins may be wiped out, that times of refreshing may come from the Lord

This is your opportunity to become a new creation in Christ and turn away from your sins and turn to God. God is the only one who is able to help you live a new life. We do not wait until we have changed to come to God. We come to God, and then He changes us. We must be willing to take the steps into change; we need to be willing to avoid certain places, break off certain relationships, close certain businesses, somethings will be easier than others, but keep this assurance that if you are willing, God will take you into seasons of refreshment.

You Need To Believe That Jesus Christ Died On The Cross And That He Is Alive

Romans 10:9
If you declare with your mouth, "Jesus is Lord," and believe in your heart that God raised him from the dead, you will be saved.

If you don't believe, then nothing really matters, the baby born of a virgin, the death on the cross and the empty grave that is not just a wonderful story; it is the gift of eternal Glory with God that has been freely given unto us, but only if we believe. John the Baptist foretold of this great light that was to come into the world and has now come; we see John telling us that many in the world will not recognise Him when he comes. But we read:

John 1:12
Yet to all who receive Him, to those who believed in His name,
He gave the right to become children of God.

Acts 16:31
They replied, "Believe in the Lord Jesus and you will be
saved–you and your household."

Acts 10:43
All the prophets testify about him that everyone who believes in
him receives forgiveness of sins through his name.

You Need To Pray To God

Romans 10:13 ...for, "Everyone who calls on the name of the Lord will be saved.

I pray that if you are reading this book and you have never received Christ into your heart, that God will fill you with the presence of the Holy Spirit, may you have the desire to accept Jesus Christ as your personal Lord and Saviour, may you pray the salvation prayer and may you discover the greatest gift you will ever receive, the gift of God's perfect love and the gift of eternal life.
Today I am asking you to put your trust in Christ and pray this prayer.

PRAYER OF SALVATION

Dear heavenly Father, I know that I am a sinner, and I ask for Your forgiveness. I believe Jesus died for my sins and rose from the dead. I turn from my sins, I repent of my sins, and I invite You to come into my heart and life. I want to trust and follow You as my Lord and Saviour. In the Mighty Name of Jesus. Amen

---

MEDITATE

Luke 6:37	Do not judge, and you will not be judged. Do not condemn, and you will not be condemned. Forgive, and you will be forgiven.
Acts 7:59-60	While they were stoning him, Stephen prayed, "Lord Jesus, receive my spirit." Then he fell on his knees and cried out, "Lord, do not hold this sin against them." When he had said this, he fell asleep.
Luke 17:3-4	So watch yourselves. "If your brother or sister sins against you, rebuke them; and if they repent, forgive them. Even if they sin against you seven times in a day andseven times come back to you saying 'I repent,' you must forgive them."
Ephesians 4:32	"Be kind and compassionate to one another, forgiving each other, just as in Christ God forgave you."
Colossians 3:13	"Bear with each other and forgive one another if any of you has a grievance against someone. Forgive as the Lord forgave you."
Psalm 86:5 "	You, Lord, are forgiving and good, abounding in love to all who call to you."
Psalm 32:1	"Blessed is the one whose transgressions are forgiven, whose sins are covered."
Hebrews 8:12	"For I will forgive their wickedness and will remember their sins no more."

MY REFLECTIONS ON FORGIVENESS

Is there any unforgiveness in me?

If yes, who do I need to forgive?

What does God require of me?

CHAPTER 4

LOVE SAYS: *I Will Heal*

Psalm 147:3
He heals the broken-hearted and binds up their wounds.

Healing means that we are made whole. Love wants you to be healed and whole. That is exactly what God's love will do for you. Healing will look different for all of us. What we need to believe is that God has the power to heal the whole person. Whether that be spiritual healing, physical healing or emotional healing.

I used to be extremely oversensitive, easily offended and cried a lot. Whenever I meet anybody that knew me as a child, the first thing they always ask is, "Is this the one who cried so much". During my teenage years and well into my early twenties, this was something I continued to struggle with, and it also caused me so much pain and loss.

The after effect of not having lived with my mom for the first few years of my life and never knowing my biological father left scars on my life. At first, I did not realise that I suffered from abandonment issues, but the enemy did, and whenever the enemy discovers that there is a part of us that might be broken, his number one mission will be to use that to destroy us, in order, to keep us from living out our God-ordained calling.

I always questioned everyone's motives and needed constant validation that their love was real and their intentions good. I was a faith-filled young woman who really loved God, but somehow, part of my heart that should have trusted people was still broken. When I look back on my life, I do see that God is always close to me, just as he promises in *Psalm 34:18, "The Lord is near to the broken-hearted and saves the crushed in spirit."* Because of His closeness, the enemy could never get complete power over me, but he was always there lurking for any opportunity to cause me to fail and often, I did fail. Although it was a few years into my walk with the Lord that healing came into this area of my life, it took a while, not because of God but because of me. I was the one who refused to confront the reasons for my behaviour. It caused my relationships with people to suffer and even for some people to walk away from me. What we do not realise is that the wound gets bigger every time we allow the enemy to take power over our lives.

I was at risk of losing yet another relationship, the one with my now husband, when I was confronted with another opportunity to be healed. I knew very soon after meeting him that he was the one I had been praying for, yet the fear of being rejected started to creep in. We were dating long distance and every time when we had plans for him to visit me, I would find myself asking him a few times in the days leading up to the weekend if he was still planning to come, all the while preparing mentally for how I would respond if he failed to come. This was something I was used to doing as a way of protecting myself. One day after he asked me why I was always questioning him. I realised that my actions showed him that I lacked trust in our relationship, while he had never given me any reason to doubt him. I felt the Holy Spirit's conviction, and I knew I had to confront the truth and seek God for complete healing, or it was going to cost me what I now know to be God's greatest gift to me this side of heaven.

When I surrendered and finally admitted that I had issues with abandonment that caused the great fear of rejection in me, I chose to forgive and move forward. I started to believe that I was good enough to be loved, God was faithful, and I discovered the glorious experience of living in freedom from fear of rejection.

Today I walk in complete wholeness. I know that I am loved and completely healed; I also know that people's rejection does not make me any less. I know that not everyone is meant to stay in my life forever. My own struggles have taught me that the way people treat me has so much more to do with their own life experiences and very little to do with my worth. It has given me a greater sense of compassion for them, and I live to share the amazing news that there is healing for them too. Being healed does not mean the enemy had given up on trying to attack me in that area still, but it does mean that I walk in victory, and I have chosen to allow God not just to be close but also to completely fight for me instead of trying to fight the enemy myself.

Do Not Stay In Your Pit!

Genesis 37:4-8

When his brothers saw that their father loved him more than any of them, they hated him and could not speak a kind word to him. Joseph had a dream, and when he told it to his brothers, they hated him all the more. He said to them, "Listen to this dream I had: We were binding sheaves of grain out in the field when suddenly my sheaf rose and stood upright, while your sheaves gathered around mine and bowed down to it. "His brothers said to him, "Do you intend to reign over us? Will you actually rule us?" And they hated him all the more because of his dream and what he had said.

Genesis 37:17-28

"They have moved on from here," the man answered. "I heard them say, 'Let's go to Dothan.'"So Joseph went after his brothers and found them near Dothan. But they saw him in the distance, and before he reached them, they plotted to kill him. "Here comes that dreamer!" they said to each other. "Come now, let's kill him and throw him into one of these cisterns and say that a ferocious animal devoured him. Then we'll see what comes of his dreams. "When Reuben heard this, he tried to rescue him from their hands. "Let's not take his life," he said. "Don't shed any blood. Throw him into this cistern here in the wilderness, but don't lay a hand on him." Reuben said this to rescue him from them and take him back to his father. So when Joseph came to his brothers, they stripped him of his robe–the ornate robe–he was wearing and they took him and threw him into the cistern. The cistern was empty; there was no water in it. As they sat down to eat their meal, they looked up and saw a caravan of Ishmaelites coming from Gilead. Their camels were loaded with spices, balm and myrrh, and they were on their way to take them down to Egypt. Judah said to his brothers, "What will we gain if we kill our brother and cover up his blood? Come, let's sell him to the Ishmaelites and not lay our hands on him; after all, he is our brother, our own flesh and blood." His brothers agreed. So when the Midianite merchants came by, his brothers pulled Joseph up out of the cistern and sold him for twenty shekels of silver to the Ishmaelites, who took him to Egypt.

Genesis 45:1-8

Then Joseph could no longer control himself before all his attendants, and he cried out, "Have everyone leave my presence!" So there was no one with Joseph when he made himself known to his brothers. And he wept so loudly that the Egyptians heard him, and Pharaoh's household heard about it. Joseph said to his brothers, "I am Joseph! Is my father still living?" But his brothers were not able to answer him, because they were terrified at his presence. Then Joseph said to his brothers, "Come close to me." When they had done so, he said, "I am your brother Joseph, the one you sold into Egypt! And now, do not be distressed and do not be angry with yourselves for selling me here, because it was to save lives that God sent me ahead of you. For two years now there has been famine in the land, and for the next five years there will be no plowing and reaping. But God sent me ahead of you to preserve for you a remnant on earth and to save your lives by a great deliverance. "So then, it was not you who sent me here, but God. He made me father to Pharaoh, lord of his entire household and ruler of all Egypt.

The life of Joseph started off very different from my own; he was the beloved son of his father, he was favoured above his brothers, and he got a revelation of being chosen by God very early in his life. But the reason that I feel a connection with Joseph is because of everything that happened to Joseph after his brothers decided to throw him into a pit and ultimately sell him as a slave.

The story of Joseph was told to me at a very young age, and I often wondered about him. How someone who had suffered so much rejection, slavery, false accusations and even imprisonment could live a life completely surrendered to God and live out his purpose as well as he did.

My sufferings seem insignificant compared to what Joseph had to go through, yet our responses to abandonment are so different. Based on his earlier favour, the very people who should have loved him the most hated him, sold him, and robbed him of the beautiful life he was sure to have had. This had the potential to send Joseph along a dark path of brokenness and bitterness.

Not Joseph! He never took his eyes off the promises of God. He was confident in God, his promise keeper, the one who never lies. He knew who he belonged to in the midst of great disappointments.

Joseph recognised that his brothers' hatred towards him was part of God's greater plan, a plan far greater than Joseph could have imagined. But what if Joseph wallowed in the patrial of his brothers, or in the fact that he was once a beloved son now in slavery and wrongly imprisoned. Joseph had many reasons to stay in the pit of his brokenness. I, for one, would not have blamed him; I would probably be sitting and agreeing with him deeper into his whole. But if he did, he would have never reached the palace; he would have never become the great ruler who saved his people.

What pit are you wallowing in at this very moment? What has caused you to be so broken that you cannot see how God will be able to heal you and bring you into complete wholeness?

As a believer, I always thought that because I am a Christian I could never let anyone see my brokenness or the wounds that my past had left on me. The thought of what people would say always came up in my heart, and so pretence became a big part of my life, and without realising it, the pretence would eventually bring its own wounds.

Ever heard of the saying 'wolf in sheep's clothing'? That is how I would describe what pretence is, we justify it, but in essence, it is a lie. The definition of pretence is "an attempt to make something that is not the case appears to be true".

It becomes so hard and almost always causes someone you love to be hurt and could cost you your relationship. I knew that I could not pretend to be healed when it came to my relationship with my future husband; it took that realisation to bring me to my knees in complete surrender. The devil who is the father of lies and has no truth in him

(John 8:44) will want you to remain there; he will keep you in that place of brokenness living with a mask if you allow him to.

When it comes to our brokenness and the wounds that we carry, it might not only be one thing. Like Joseph, it could be a build-up of a lot of hurt, and it looks very different for all of us. But the one thing that remains the same is that God's love for us says that we are healed by the wounds of Jesus Christ, who died on the cross for our sins.

Like Joseph, we need to walk steadfastly in the promises of God, not in the reality of our circumstances; if we can only open our spiritual eyes, we might get the revelation that our current hardship is the stepping stone to the greater plan God has for us.

I could not have imagined that God would allow my children to be born within the constitution of marriage with a loving, wonderful father, something that seemed so foreign to me growing up.

Isaiah 53:5

But he was pierced for our transgressions, he was crushed for our iniquities; the punishment that brought us peace was on him, and by his wounds we are healed.

Healing came for me only when I acknowledged to God that I was broken and had wounds that needed his healing touch. When we are physically sick and have tried all the home remedies, but keep getting worse, we must go to the doctor, and when we arrive, we will be asked what is wrong, and then they will prescribe something for you that will help make you better.

Getting healed by God works in the same way. First, you need to say it to God and sometimes even someone physical that you can trust, and then you need to do everything that God is telling you to.
The good news I have for you today is that nothing is too big for God to heal, He wants you to be whole, and after you first accept the unconditional love of God and you believe that love is not what God does, it is who He is, this is how you can start to walk in freedom and receive complete healing from God.

Confess Your Sins, Believe That You Are Forgiven And Forgive Others!

James 5:16
Therefore, confess your sins to each other and pray for each other so that you may be healed. The prayer of a righteous person is powerful and effective.

Psalm 103:12
as far as the east is from the west,
so far has he removed our transgressions from us.

Healing and forgiveness go hand in hand. If you think about it, most of the things that have caused us bitterness and brokenness were either because of our sins or our inability to forgive the ones that have hurt us. Joseph had enough reason to never ever speak to his brothers again; I mean, they wanted to kill him, but what would have happened had Joseph decided to live with a heart of unforgiveness and bitterness. He would have lived a life of brokenness, and many would have suffered because they needed Joseph to be standing boldly in his calling, that provided for his people in a time when they needed provision.

Just as we cannot be forgiven by God if we do not forgive others, unforgiveness will also keep us sick! Forgiveness is what Christ brought on the cross, and forgiveness is what will bring complete healing to all of us.
Completely forgive all the people who have hurt you! Stop blaming others for your current problems; remember that your attitude belongs to you. Never let your reason for your pain become your excuse for the broken life you continue to live.

Romans 12:21
Do not be overcome by evil, but overcome evil with good.

Pray and have Faith!

James 5:15
And a prayer offered in faith will make the sick person well; the Lord will raise them up. If they have sinned, they will be forgiven.

Prayer is our communication to God; the Bible also says they have not because they asked not. For prayers to be answered, we need to have faith that God can do what we are believing before Him.

The woman with the issue of blood went out to seek Jesus; she believed that all she needed to do was touch his garment, that was faith, and we read that Jesus says to her, *"Daughter, your faith has healed you. Go in peace and be freed from your suffering" (Mark 5:34).*

Those days people could go out and physically seek Jesus's presence. Today we might not have that privilege, but we have our own privilege to be able to go to God in prayer at any time that we want to.

We need to have the same faith and desire just to touch Jesus and come to Him in prayer with faith; then, we will be healed and receive freedom and peace.

Stay In God's Word!

Psalms 119:105
Your word is a lamp for my feet, a light on my path.

Now more than ever we need to stay in the word of God. The enemy is not about to stop his attacks on you just because you have received God's healing; in fact, he will work overtime to see you fall again. We need to be reading the word daily.

When we pray, we are talking to God, and when we read the Bible, God is talking to us; the more we get to know God, the stronger our faith will grow. If we do not read the word daily, we are missing an opportunity to hear God speak. We are living in a time when we do not have the luxury of saying we do not need to enquire of the Lord. If you need healing, you need the word! Put the word of God in your mouth and keep confessing it over your life.

Let The Holy Spirit Lead Your Life!

John 14:16-17
And I will ask the Father, and he will give you another advocate to help you and be with you forever–the Spirit of truth. The world cannot accept him because it neither sees him nor knows him. But you know him, for he lives with you and will be in you.

The Holy Spirit will lead you in all truth, you cannot fight the principalities of the darkness in your own strength, and God did not leave us alone he gave us His Holy Spirit! The Holy Spirit of God gives gifts to the children of God, and one of the gifts is the gift of healing. God distributes the gift of healing according to His will, *God also testified to it by signs, wonders and various miracles, and by gifts of the Holy Spirit distributed according to his will (Hebrews 2:4).* If you allow the Holy Spirit to lead you, you will witness signs and wonders and miracles.

Get Up And Go!

John 5:8
Then Jesus said to Him: "Get up! Pick up your mat and walk."

When we have been healed, we need to walk in that healing boldly. We need to remember that we have not been healed only for ourselves, but have been made whole, and we need to share this with everyone that will listen.

We have been put on this earth for a specific purpose; we have been set free by the redemption of the cross. We have been healed by Love, and we must share the healing Love of God with everyone we encounter. We are the hands and feet of Jesus here on earth. Our testimony of healing will bring hope and healing to the sick.

Galatians 6:2
Carry each other's burdens, and in this way you will fulfill the law of Christ.

The word of God is the most powerful weapon you have to fight attacks from the enemy. Therefore, I encourage you to meditate on the following Scriptures if you are struggling with any of the below; I pray that God will open the eyes of your heart and that the healing power of God will penetrate your heart as you start to believe in the healing power of the words that God left for us in His word. Healing belongs to you, in the Mighty name of Jesus!

MEDITATE

Spiritually Healing

Jeremiah 3:22	Return, faithless people; I will cure you of backsliding." "Yes, we will come to you, for you are the LORD our God.
1 Peter 2:24	"He himself bore our sins" in his body on the cross, so that we might die to sins and live for righteousness; "by his wounds you have been healed."

Physically Healing

Psalm 103:2-3	Praise the Lord, my soul, and forget not all his benefits– who forgives all your sins and heals all your diseases.
Psalm 41:3	The LORD sustains them on their sickbed and restores them from their bed of illness.

Emotional Healing

Psalm 34:18	The LORD is close to the brokenhearted and saves those who are crushed in spirit.
Psalm 107:19-20	Then they cried to the LORD in their trouble, and he saved them from their distress. He sent out his word and healed them; he rescued them from the grave.

MY REFLECTIONS ON GOD'S HEALING

Do I need God's healing power?

If yes, what do I require healing from?

What does God require of me?

CHAPTER 5

LOVE SAYS:
I Will Restore

Joel 2: 25-26
"I will repay you for the years the locusts have eaten— the great locust and the young locust, the other locusts and the locust swarm— my great army that I sent among you. You will have plenty to eat, until you are full, and you will praise the name of the Lord your God, who has worked wonders for you; never again will my people be shamed.

I was born to a single mother who, at the age of twenty, was basically still touching the borders of being a teenager. Like a lot of grandparents in our communities do, my mother's father and mother looked after me for the first six years of my life, then my grandmother passed away suddenly just before my seventh birthday.

The next three years would see me living between my grandfather and my mother's sister. I was ten years old when I went to live with my mom permanently. The life there was very different to the one I knew living with my grandparents.

In this season of my life, I was exposed to the abuse that my mom endured, and our relationship at that point needed a foundation, the years away from my mom had left its scars. We struggled greatly to connect, and, for many years, I found myself questioning if she really loved me. I had always felt that somehow, she loved my brother and sister more than me. These feelings that I was struggling with were the cause of many misunderstandings between my mother and I, which left me in tears and feeling more rejected every time; it was almost as if the scars were just being deepened. I love my mother so much and have always just wanted validation from her. I would learn later that it also had a lot to do with the fact that one of my main loves in languages are words of affirmation.

When I first became a born-again believer in Jesus Christ, and I discovered the power of prayer and the truth of God's word, I knew that God could save my mother's life, which would mean restoration for our relationship. I was a thirteen-year-old teenager who was very much still living with the faith of a young child, so to me, this just seemed like the natural results that would come when my mother got saved.

I started praying very earnestly for my mother's salvation. I expected it to happen overnight. But weeks became months and eventually years. It would be three years of prayer and holding onto my faith; I never stopped believing that I would get what I was asking God for.

When I was sixteen years old, my mother got radically saved. The way she lived changed completely, and so did our lives, not for the better from outward appearances, and the immediate restoration of our relations I had hoped for and asked God for did not come. In fact, the years to come was very much a wilderness season for our family.

And our relationships continue to struggle. We struggled because the feeling of being less loved would not leave me. I remember praying for God to restore our relationship. Many years and many moments of disagreement and blame went by. The expectation that our connections would just be instant now that we were both saved was not met.

It would take many more years, and I was in my early twenties when restoration did come. And when it came, it was as beautiful as I imagined it would be. It took a serious conversation where truth was spoken by both of us, and a new understanding was brought to light as we were able to really listen and really speak. Our hearts were ready, and finally, in a moment, years of hurt, confusion, and misunderstandings were healed.

For us, it required speaking the truth in love and forgiving hearts; I am a firm believer that when we bring things to light, we take hold of the enemy, and therefore we are set free. We both needed to forgive, and to be forgiven, we both were set free.

At that moment, I finally had the relationship with my mother that I had always dreamed of. In fact, it has been so much better than I imagined and even prayed for, just like the Bible says.

Ephesians 3:20
Now to him who is able to do immeasurably more than all we ask or imagine, according to his power that is at work within us.

The next part of our journey was one that only God himself could have designed. We became the best of friends; her life is the single most visible example to me that our God is alive and that He loves us so much. I see her love, and I feel her love, and God gave us a good couple of years of just being her and me before I met my husband. In those years, we built such a solid foundation of love and trust. Today she is the person I most want to be like.

The enemy had stolen the first ten years of my life with my mom, and he used what happened in those years to steal the next ten years, and I allowed him to do it. I know that had it not been for my relationship with God and my believing the truths of His word. The truth is that He loves me and promises to restore even the broken things and make them new. I might never have experienced the amazing relationship I now have with my mom. That is the love that restores.

When we come to Christ, all of us brings with us something that we feel we lost. Our sin will do that because when we live in sin, the enemy will always use our sinful nature to destroy the beautiful things God blessed us with. He will use those things to remind us that we do not deserve the love of God. But what he did not bargain on is that God already said that He will restore everything and not just restore, but give back plenty. I am eternally grateful to be a testament to this.

Underserving Lost

Sometimes our losses are so great, and sometimes it might seem so undeserving, and it may have nothing to do with sin; it can become hard to believe that God will one day restore and everything will be beautiful again.

Job was one such man who had to face unimaginable loss because of his faithfulness to God. It did not seem fair for Job to have to suffer as much as he did, but as we see in the Scriptures that the enemy has no intentions of letting us live in peace ever. He came to steal, kill and destroy, and for a moment in Job's life, it looks as if the enemy had managed to completely destroy Job. In all human abilities, it did not seem possible for anyone to come out of such immense loss with their faith and hope still so strong that God will be able to restore their life.

Job 1:7-19
The LORD said to Satan, "Where have you come from?" Satan answered the LORD, "From roaming throughout the earth, going back and forth on it." Then the LORD said to Satan, "Have you considered my servant Job? There is no one on earth like him; he is blameless and upright, a man who fears God and shuns evil." "Does Job fear God for nothing?" Satan replied. "Have you not put a hedge around him and his household and everything he has? You have blessed the work of his hands, so that his flocks and herds are spread throughout the land. But now stretch out your hand and strike everything he has, and he will surely curse you to your face." The LORD said to Satan, "Very well, then, everything he has is in your power, but on the man himself do not lay a finger." Then Satan went out from the presence of the LORD. One day when Job's sons and daughters were feasting and drinking wine at the oldest brother's house, a messenger came to Job and said, "The oxen were plowing and the donkeys were grazing nearby, and the Sabeans attacked and made off with them. They put the servants to the sword, and I am the only one who has escaped to tell you!" While he was still speaking, another messenger came and said, "The fire of God fell from the heavens and burned up the sheep and the servants, and I am the only one who has escaped to tell you!" While he was still speaking, another messenger came and said, "The Chaldeans formed three raiding parties and swept down on your camels and made off with them. They put the servants to the sword, and I am the only one who has escaped to tell you!" While he was still speaking, yet another messenger came and said, "Your sons and daughters were feasting and drinking wine at the oldest brother's house, when suddenly a mighty wind swept in from the desert and struck the four corners of the house. It collapsed on them and they are dead, and I am the only one who has escaped to tell you!" At this, Job got up and tore his robe and shaved his head. Then he fell to the ground in worship and said: "Naked I came from my mother's womb, and naked I will depart. The LORD gave and the LORD has taken away; may the name of the LORD be praised." In all this, Job did not sin by charging God with wrongdoing.

The account of Job's great loss is certainly tragic and very sad, yet in all this, Job did not sin in charging God with wrongdoing. I believe that the only reason that Job was able to do this is that He knew who his God was, He knew that God is love, and just like Abraham, when tasked with sacrificing Isaac, he knew that God was able to bring everything he lost back to life, he had to hold onto his faith.

God requires that we fully believe in the promises that He gives us and that He is able to fully restore everything and so much more than we can think or ask. Nevertheless, we can take some valuable life lessons from the life of Job.

The Bad Things That Happened To You Are Not Always Because Of Your Sins

Job 1:1
In the land of Uz there lived a man whose name was Job. This man was blameless and upright; he feared God and shunned evil.

Sometimes the very desire we have in our hearts to live righteously before God and serve Him well will be enough reason for the enemy to want us to suffer to get us to sin and walk away from our salvation. So examine your own heart and seek God.

In Every Situation, Always Remain Hopeful

Job 13:15
Though he slay me, yet will I hope in him; I will surely defend my ways to his face.

Remaining hopeful in the midst of hardship or loss or tragedy that is a direct result that living for God can be the hardest thing, but let us keep our eyes on the Lord and His word. (*1 Peter 3:17 - For it is better, if it is God's will, to suffer for doing good than for doing evil.)* let us follow the example of Job and continue to hope in God and restoration will surely come.

Man Will Fail Us, But God Never Does

Job 16:2
I have heard many things like these, you are miserable comforters, all of you!

Job 19:25-27
I know that my redeemer lives, and that in the end he will stand on the earth. And after my skin has been destroyed, yet in my flesh I will see God, I myself will see him with my own eyes–I, and not another. How my heart yearns within me!

People are humans. All of us are born into a world of sin. Because of this, we can never expect that in life we will not be disappointed by someone. Yes, it might happen, but if we learn to depend on God more and on people less, we will reduce the risk of disappointment, unforgiveness and years of pain and loss, but if we have gone down that road already, we thank God for the loving gift of restoration.

God Is In Control Of Our Lives

Job 1:12
The Lord said to Satan, "Very well, then, everything he has is in your power, but on the man himself do not lay a finger. "Then Satan went out from the presence of the Lord."

As a daughter of the Most High King, you can rest in this knowledge that God holds the power of your life in His hands. This does not mean that we will never see hardship because the word also tells us that in this world we will have many troubles, but we have hope because the Lord has overcome this world, and He that is in us is greater than him who is on the world and God as authority over the enemy always!

He was always there. I am not saying you are not allowed to be angry for a moment at your situation. I am saying that you have the promise of restoration the moment you chose the love of God in all its fullness, and that means that what you will gain will be more than what you have lost.

Job 42:12
The LORD blessed the latter part of Job's life more than the former part. He had fourteen thousand sheep, six thousand camels, a thousand yoke of oxen and a thousand donkeys.

Job 42:10
And God did restore and Bless Job as we see in the word "After Job had prayed for his friends, the LORD restored his fortunes and gave him twice as much as he had before."

Job 23:10-12
But he knows the way that I take, when he has tested me, I will come forth as gold. My feet have closely followed his steps; I have kept to his way without turning aside. I have not departed from the commands of his lips; I have treasured the words of his mouth more than my daily bread.

Sometimes we might not understand why God seems to be so far away during the hardest times in our lives, but when we look back on seasons past, we see that He was always with us. We can rest in the knowledge that God is in control of our lives. The victory on the cross is evidence that no matter what happens to us, God has already won the victory. We have the victory over the enemy. In your times of trouble, hold onto the hope that God will restore He is the one in control.

MEDITATE

1 Peter 5:10	And the God of all grace, who called you to his eternal glory in Christ, after you have suffered a little while, will himself restore you and make you strong, firm and steadfast.
Psalm 51:12	Restore to me the joy of your salvation and grant me a willing spirit, to sustain me.
Isaiah 61:7	Instead of your shame you will receive a double portion, and instead of disgrace you will rejoice in your inheritance. And so, you will inherit a double portion in your land, and everlasting joy will be yours.
Zachariah 9:12	Return to your fortress, you prisoners of hope; even now I announce that I will restore twice as much to you.
Amos 9:14	And I will bring my people Israel back from exile. "They will rebuild the ruined cities and live in them. They will plant vineyards and drink their wine; they will make gardens and eat their fruit.
Hosea 6:1	Come, let us return to the Lord. He has torn us to pieces but he will heal us, he has injured us but he will bind up our wounds.

MY REFLECTIONS ON RESTORATION

What have I lost?

What is my role in all this?

What does God require of me?

CHAPTER 6

LOVE SAYS:
I Will Provide

Matthew 6:25-26
Therefore I tell you, do not worry about your life, what you will eat or drink; or about your body, what you will wear. Is not life more than food, and the body more than clothes? Look at the birds of the air; they do not sow or reap or store away in barns, and yet your heavenly Father feeds them. Are you not much more valuable than they?

When I accepted God as my Father and committed my life to Him, I could not have imagined how greatly His love would provide for my needs.

I knew at a very young age what I wanted to do when I grew up. I think I was about sixteen years old when I decided that I wanted to become a missionary; I would go into the mission field and preach the uncompromised word of God. My fire for the gospel burned brightly, and I had a hunger for the word.

When I finished high school, I was set to go to Bible College. All I had was faith and my Bible (a beautiful new one gifted to me by my local church). I had no doubt that this was God's will for my life, so I did not consider doing anything else.

The week I was set to leave, the course of my life took a very different turn. As I was making my plans to go to Bible College, my mom and dad were going through a breakup and life in Gauteng was becoming really hard to the point where we had no other choice but to leave, so we sold everything we had and together with my mom, brother and sister we got on a train to Cape Town with only the clothes we owned and a box of plates and moved to Cape Town to live with my grandfather.

At 18 years old, I needed to find a job, as we had no means of income. My mother struggled to find a job. My sister and brother were both still in school. I eventually found a job as a cashier, earning just enough to keep the four of us going. To say that I was extremely confused by what had happened would be an understatement. I think I automatically assumed that wanting to go into the mission field is the noblest thing, and how could God not provide for me to do that. I really had to lay before God to get an understanding, but the revelations would not come for a long time.

All I knew was that what I was doing at the time, cannot be the hopeful future that God had promised. So I prayed and asked God to please provide for me to get some sort of education so that I could get a better job. This was an impossible request as, at the time, we were basically living on the little money I was earning as a cashier.

In faith, I started to apply to colleges and was accepted for a diploma in financial management. I figured that I could save some money for my registration and trusted God would provide the tuition fees.

Unfortunately, saving money proved impossible as I was earning just about enough to keep us going. This resulted in me not having the registration fees the week I was to leave for college.

I knew that it would require a miracle from God, one I was praying for and really believing God would provide. I was set to leave on the Monday and the Saturday my cousin came to our house to let me know that God had instructed her to help me with the registration fees. Even though I had many thoughts in my heart of how God might come through this, one did not come up. In this, I learned a valuable lesson that as well-intended as my plan to save money was, we do not need to think up ideas for God, we need to trust Him and He will lead us in the right direction or send someone He instructed to act in obedience to His purpose concerning our life. God's word says many are the plans of a man's heart, but it's the Lord's purpose that prevails (Proverbs 19:21)

At the age of 19 years old, I started college. I did not know that going off on my own would put such a big spotlight on my relationship with Christ. I knew He loved me, but this for me was the time that I realised my love for God was true. Being that young, with so much freedom, proved to be a test of my true intentions and my heart towards the God I proclaimed to love.

As I started this new journey, I had to keep God's word constantly before my eyes *(Keep this Book of the Law always on your lips; meditate on it day and night, so that you may be careful to do everything written in it. Then you will be prosperous and successful. Joshua 1:8)* and remind myself that if it had not been for my heavenly Father's great provision, I would not be there *(If the LORD had not been on our side–let Israel say– Psalm 124:1).* This kept my heart focused on Him, and I set out with

the intention to bring Him Glory.
This turned out to be a season that would grow my faith and love for God to a new level. So, once again, just like when we moved to Cape Town the year before, I started my journey with a bag of clothes, God, and the faith that He will supply all my needs.

By this time, my mom was able to find a job cleaning houses. The money she earned was just enough to keep the three of them going. This meant that she did not have anything to give to me. From time to time, my grandfather, who was a pensioner, would help me with some necessities.

I worked hard at my studies and did very well. After the first six months, I was among the top achievers in my class, but I was also behind with the tuition payments that semester. With this happening, I realised that I would not be able to come back the following semester if God did not perform another miracle, and my mom and I started praying for one. We applied to a bank for a student loan, but because I had no one who had a permanent job to stand in as guarantor. My cousin offered to, but I was declined as she was already guarantor for her sister's approved student loan.

I was devastated at that no, which I thought this was going to be the answer. The day I was supposed to leave for our holiday break, I remember being sick with flu and one of my lecturers telling me about a possible bursary; she mentioned that the due date for the application might be closed already but that I should try, as my marks were very good. I dragged my sick self to the administration office and completed my application.

During my break at home, we got the call that the bursary was approved but only for my class fees, not for any living expenses and because of this, they were reluctant to give me the bursary. We had to convince them that I would sort out my living arrangements before they approved the bursary. Even though we did not have a solution, we promised that we would sort it out, and in good faith, they gave me the bursary.

The most affordable solutions to my living arrangement seem to be me finding someplace off-campus at someone's house. I was not very keen on this as I knew how difficult it would be to live with strange people. However, I did the only thing I knew to do and asked God to please provide a way for me to stay in the hostel. I have always had the boldness to share my heart with God, and I believe that He is concerned about the little things.

I started the second semester hopeful. The head of the hostel offered to let me stay for one month to give me time to sort out my finances or alternative arrangements. As the end of the one month's grace period was approaching, I was just spiritually at a very low point. My faith was slipping. I was always the one with nothing, I was always the one who was questioned about why I wore the same outfit if we had a special event at college. Every day I was living by faith for everything I needed, and I was tired. I remember one Tuesday morning during my quiet time with the Lord, I could not pray, I mustered up the words and pleaded with God to give me a lifeline, to just do one thing that will show me He had not forgotten about me, and I went to class.

On that same day, after one of my classes, myself and two other students were called to stay behind; we were informed that we had to meet the college's rector in his office the Friday morning. I knew immediately, without knowing what it would be, that this was the lifeline that I was waiting on God for.

When I entered the boardroom that Friday morning, I could not have dreamed up the outcome of that meeting. Sitting across from me at the round table, the rector informed us that a German company had decided to give bursaries to the top four students in my course. This bursary was the first of its sort in the history of the college. When I heard the amount, I was stunned because God provided the full year's tuition, living cost included in one instant. The rector excused himself from the room and returned to inform us that it was tuition for both years. I was so blown away I had asked God for a lifeline, and He gave me a red sea kind of miracle.

At 19 years of age, God was starting to give me glimpses of what promise land living could be like for me if I would just choose to trust Him with all my heart.

This turned out to be the season of my life that I got to truly see the love that provides. Of course, it did not always come in big, bold miracles like that day in the boardroom, but it did always come whenever I needed it.

God Is Our Only Source!

1 Kings 17:2-16

Then the word of the Lord came to Elijah: "Leave here, turn eastward and hide in the Kerith Ravine, east of the Jordan. You will drink from the brook, and I have directed the ravens to supply you with food there." So he did what the Lord had told him. He went to the Kerith Ravine, east of the Jordan, and stayed there. The ravens brought him bread and meat in the morning and bread and meat in the evening, and he drank from the brook. Then the word of the Lord came to him:

"Go at once to Zarephath in the region of Sidon and stay there. I have directed a widow there to supply you with food." So he went to Zarephath. When he came to the town gate, a widow was there gathering sticks. He called to her and asked, "Would you bring me a little water in a jar so I may have a drink?" As she was going to get it, he called, "And bring me, please, a piece of bread." "As surely as the Lord your God lives," she replied, "I don't have any bread—only a handful of flour in a jar and a little olive oil in a jug. I am gathering a few sticks to take home and make a meal for myself and my son, that we may eat it—and die." Elijah said to her, "Don't be afraid. Go home and do as you have said. But first make a small loaf of bread for me from what you have and bring it to me, and then make something for yourself and your son. For this is what the Lord, the God of Israel, says: 'The jar of flour will not be used up and the jug of oil will not run dry until the day the Lord sends rain on the land.' She went away and did as Elijah had told her. So there was food every day for Elijah and for the woman and her family. For the jar of flour was not used up and the jug of oil did not run dry, in keeping with the word of the Lord spoken by Elijah.

As a parent, I see how my children naturally expect us to provide for their needs. Imagine if we had the same natural gravitation towards God, unfortunately, as humans, we do not, and until we understand that God wants us to know that He is our only source and He does not compete with anyone else, we will always find ourselves coming short as we make our own plans and place our dependence on other things. Of course, God can use these things too, but if not given to us as a resource by God, it will hold no supernatural power, and what God could have done in a moment will take us so much longer, and even then we will still find ourselves in lack.

When we look at the life of the prophet Elijah we see that during a great famine in the land, God provided for Elijah in miraculous ways, and the things and people that God used certainly would not come up in the heart of Elijah if he had to make his own plans.

The brook, the ravens and the widow that fed Elijah were all resources provided through God, the source that gave the miraculous power. The resources that God uses may change, but if we hold onto Him as our source, the changing of the resources should not steer us unto a path of fear.

Just like God changed the resources for Elijah, God first used my cousin to get me to college and then God used local and international bursaries as the resources to provide for me. The loan was a resource that I came up with in my own human capacity, but because it was not connected to the power of my only source, God, it caused me disappointment that I could have avoided if I decided to stay connected to my God. The how and the when is not for us to concern ourselves with; we need to focus on what is required in order for us to experience the Love that provides in all its fullness.

Through my own experience and the life of Elijah, I discovered that there are three important things that we need to do.

We Need To Have Faith

Without faith, it is impossible to please God; we can do nothing if we do not have faith in our source. Having faith that God can provide in all you need will produce in you the confidence to come to God to ask for His help if you do not have confidence in the love that says He will provide in all you need and you do not ask, you will not get anything from God. God does not require a mountain size faith from us; in fact, he says that we only need faith as small as a mustard seed in order for Him to perform a mountain size miracle, on that morning in my college room when I cried out for a lifeline, I was also holding onto a mustard seed size faith, and it was enough.

Hebrews 11:6

And without faith it is impossible to please God, because anyone who comes to him must believe that he exists and that he rewards those who earnestly seek him.

We Need To Obey God

Twice God gave Elijah instructions that did not make sense. For example, how can a raven provide food for a person, and how will a poor widow be able to feed Elijah. But we do not see Elijah question God; He only obeyed when God said go. When we find ourselves in a place of lack of obedience, God will always bring provision. We need to remember that to live in obedience to God, we need to have a relationship with God where we are able to hear His voice in order for us to know what He is commanding us to do.

Jeremiah 7:23

but I gave them this command: Obey me, and I will be your God and you will be my people. Walk in obedience to all I command you, that it may go well with you.

We Need To Have A Giving Heart

Having a generous heart will automatically become a part of who you are when you walk in the fullness of who God has called you to be. In the Kingdom of God, we see that the whole Bible is centred around the concept of sowing and reaping. We cannot expect to receive from God if we are never willing to sow into the Kingdom of God. This is not limited to you giving your monthly tithes. It will always come back to us living in a relationship with and in obedience to God, so that we are in a position to follow His commands. When God provided for Elijah, He was also at the same time providing for the poor widow. Sometimes

God will require us to do something first to see if we will trust Him. The widow was required to first make Elijah some bread even though she only had enough for one meal for her family. When she did, God provided enough for all of them.

Proverbs 11:25
A generous person will prosper;
whoever refreshes others will be refreshed.

God is faithful in His promises. And when He says He loves us, we need to know that love always provides for the needs of those who are His. It will require faith from you; it will ask you to boldly live for Jesus Christ even when the world may look at you and question why you are not as prosperous as they are.

I pray that as you stand in front of your red sea today, with nowhere to turn, that you may turn your eyes towards heaven to the Lord your God. May you know in your heart that God is able to provide exceedingly and abundantly above all you can think or ask. May you be bold in your faith, be committed to living in obedience to God, giving with a joyful heart, even if it is all you have and may you be confident in knowing that you can ask God anything and He will make way for you!

MEDITATE

James 4:2	You desire but do not have, so you kill. You covet but you cannot get what you want, so you quarrel and fight. You do not have because you do not ask God.
Mark 11:24	Therefore, I tell you, whatever you ask for in prayer, believe that you have received it, and it will be yours.
James 1:6	But when you ask, you must believe and not doubt, because the one who doubts is like a wave of the sea, blown and tossed by the wind.
Psalm 37:4	Take delight in the LORD, and he will give you the desires of your heart.
Psalm 34:9	Fear the LORD, you his holy people, for those who fear him lack nothing.
Deut 24:19	When you are harvesting in your field and you overlook a sheaf, do not go back to get it. Leave it for the foreigner, the fatherless and the widow, so that the LORD your God may bless you in all the work of your hands.
Luke 6:38	Give, and it will be given to you. A good measure, pressed down, shaken together and running over, will be poured into your lap. For with the measure you use, it will be measured to you."

MY REFLECTIONS ON PROVISION

Do you have a need that God has not been providing in?

What does God require of you?

CHAPTER 7

LOVE SAYS: *I Will Protect*

2 Thessalonians 3:3
But the Lord is faithful, and he will strengthen you and protect you from the evil one.

One of the most amazing things about our God is that He protects us from everything, even the things we do not know we needed protection from.

Let me share this with you I started praying for my husband when I was only 14 years old. When I became a believer and got the revelation that we can ask anything in the name of Jesus, I was adamant that I would seek his advice Him about everything,

I have always had a desire that one day I would have my own family, and it would be the way God intended. Because I believed that God knew who my husband would be, my prayer was always very specific towards Him as a person.

It would go something like this: *God, I pray for my future husband I know You know who he is and what he is doing right now, I pray for his protection, I pray that he will know you and serve you, I pray that you will give him wisdom in all his decisions.* Of course, as I got older and more mature, the prayer evolved with me, but I continued to pray very specifically for that person.

At the age of 28, I was still very much single and yes, there were days that I wondered if God was ever going to send this man that I had been praying for, for almost 15 years. Then the day finally came, or so I thought. He was clothed in sheep's clothing; hence, it took knowing the voice of God very clearly that would save me.

An apostle that we had known for a while had a revelation that God had shown her who my husband was, and she shared this with us. I was intrigued as I never expected God to do it that way. But I must admit that I felt a bit flattered that God would be so specific. She shared a bit about who he was, summed up he was a born-again believer, financially very well off, and he had two children.

I will not lie; the fact that he had children threw me off at first. I had gone home that night and spoke to God about it. When I started praying for my husband at 14 years old, I also made a very important decision to save myself for marriage so, at the age of 28, I was still a virgin because I kept myself pure, and my heart's desire was that my husband and I would have our own family together, this was difficult for me to understand. But by this time in my life, I knew who my God was, and I knew that if this was His choice for me, that I would find the happiness that I desired and prayed for.

After we (my mom and I prayed it), I agreed to meet him. The first time I met him, there was no immediate attraction; in fact, I saw the first warning sign that this might not be God that same night, as I discovered that he did not have two children but three. This made me wonder about how well the apostle knew this man, but he asked me out on a formal date, and I agreed to go.

The one thing that was highlighted when I was told about him was how financially well off he was, and indeed he showed up with some fancy cars at the first meeting, and when we went on our first official date. The night ended up being one of the worst experiences I had ever had; I made sure to pay for my own meal, as I could not bring myself to qualify it as a date. The reason I am saying it was really bad was because of the realisation in those moments that this was not God, and immediately I knew that it had to be a distraction from the enemy. I felt really insulted that the enemy thought that I could be deceived by money. In the natural, this guy would most probably be able to give me a life with beautiful and expensive things, but that has never been where my heart was, and I realised that the enemy will try anything to keep us from God's greatest gifts if we lose our focus.

That night I could hardly sleep. Then my mother confirmed that she also had confirmation in her heart that this man was not God sent. I was shaken to my core, mostly as the revelations came from someone who proclaimed to really walk with God, but when we shared with her that God had given us a different revelation. Her response was even more shocking, she was adamant that she heard God correctly, but also boldly stated that I did not have to marry him should I not want to. At that moment, the Holy Spirit confirmed that this was not His will for me. I knew that my God is not a man that would lie and say one thing and mean something else, so I walked away.

About two weeks later, I met my future husband, and I instantly knew that it was him. As I got to know him, he would tell me stories of moments when he was in danger and how he would be protected, and I knew that those were the moments when I was praying for him. I realised that the enemy tried to lure me into another relationship with the promise of money and material things, he was preying on the lack of things we needed, and he used someone that stood in spiritual authority over people. Had I not known God for myself and lived in the shadow of the Almighty, I know for sure that a marriage with that man would have cost me a lot. Not everything that looks like God is God, the Bible says in *1 John 4:1, "Dear friends, do not believe every spirit, but test the spirits to see whether they are from God, because many false prophets have gone out into the world."*

My Refuge And My Fortress

Psalm 91
Whoever dwells in the shelter of the Most High
will rest in the shadow of the Almighty.
I will say of the Lord, "He is my refuge and my fortress,
my God, in whom I trust. "Surely he will save you
from the fowler's snare
and from the deadly pestilence.
He will cover you with his feathers,
and under his wings you will find refuge;
his faithfulness will be your shield and rampart.
You will not fear the terror of night,
nor the arrow that flies by day,
nor the pestilence that stalks in the darkness,
nor the plague that destroys at midday.
A thousand may fall at your side,

ten thousand at your right hand,
but it will not come near you.
You will only observe with your eyes
and see the punishment of the wicked.
If you say, "The Lord is my refuge,"
and you make the Most High your dwelling,
no harm will overtake you,
no disaster will come near your tent.
For he will command his angels concerning you
to guard you in all your ways;
they will lift you up in their hands,
so that you will not strike your foot against a stone.
You will tread on the lion and the cobra;
you will trample the great lion and the serpent.
"Because he[b] loves me," says the Lord, "I will rescue him;
I will protect him, for he acknowledges my name.
He will call on me, and I will answer him;
I will be with him in trouble,
I will deliver him and honor him.
With long life I will satisfy him
and show him my salvation."

When we accept God as our Father, and we start living in His love, and we choose to dwell in His presence, His protection will follow us all the days of our lives. Sometimes we do not even know that we need protection from something or someone, but we have the promise in God's word that the Holy Spirit will make known to us the secret things of God. He is all-knowing and all-powerful; you want him as your advocate and guide.

The one thing that you do have to realise is that you still get to choose if you want the protection of God. God will never force us to do anything; we are loved by Him, there is no condition to that, the only thing that keeps you from living in the fullness of all that comes with His love is you. Will you choose to accept it and everything that comes with being loved by the Most High God. Will you choose His protection? If you say yes, you will do what is required by the word of God.

Stay in God's Presence

As the word says that we hide under the shelter of the Almighty, it says that God will allow His angels to encamp around us. This means that we need to be found in His presence to be surrounded by His angels. We need to remove ourselves from those toxic friendships or toxic romantic relationships. We cannot think it is ok, to continue to move in the same places that caused us hurt or caused us to be in dangerous situations, and then expect God to protect us there.

I am talking about every area of your life, whether it be protecting your heart or your physical body or your belongings, God is your ever-present help in time of need. So we have to constantly remind ourselves that we have the amazing privilege of having access to God Almighty. When we accept Jesus Christ into our hearts, we have the gift of the Holy Spirit and we can ask for help at any time. God will always answer us, and if we do whatever He says, He will help us out of our trouble and He promises to honour us and satisfy us with a long life.

As a child of the Almighty God, we get to rest in the knowledge that God's protection is for us all the days of our lives; I pray that you will find peace that surpasses all understanding as you remind yourself of who and how you are protected by.

You Have The Eyes Of God On You

2 Chronicles 16:9

For the eyes of the Lord range throughout the earth to strengthen those whose hearts are fully committed to him. You have done a foolish thing, and from now on you will be at war."

God is always watching over you, and you can rest in the knowledge that nothing on earth happens outside of the sight of God.

You have your own army

2 Kings 6:17

And Elisha prayed, "Open his eyes, LORD, so that he may see." Then the LORD opened the servant's eyes, and he looked and saw the hills full of horses and chariots of fire all around Elisha.

God's angels surround us, ready to rescue us at the command of the Lord; we have no reason to live in fear or live a limited life!

You Have Hedges Of Protection Around You

Job 1:10

"Have you not put a hedge around him and his household and everything he has? You have blessed the work of his hands, so that his flocks and herds are spread throughout the land.

The amazing thing about this promise is that God does not only put a hedge around us, but also our family and our possessions. God will never leave His children exposed! He knows that the enemy's number one task is to steal, kill and destroy, He will protect the abundant life He promises for us (John 10:10).

You Have The Holy Spirit!

Romans 8:14
For those who are led by the Spirit of God are the children of God.

The presence of the Holy Spirit is our greatest gift that Jesus left us when He went up to heaven. Had it not been for the sure conviction of the Holy Spirit, then I am sure I would either be divorced, or very unhappy had I married that man. The Holy Spirit will always lead us to do the right thing, and to go in the right direction.

You Have The Power Of The Blood Of Jesus

Revelations 12:11 They triumphed over him
by the blood of the Lamb and by the word of their testimony;
they did not love their lives so much as to shrink from death.

It is by the Blood and only the Blood of Jesus that we receive redemption and the gift of eternal life. The Blood of Jesus holds all power, authority and is incomparable. The Blood of Jesus is the secret to our victory, the Blood of Jesus on the doorpost of the Israelites houses protected them, and in the same way, we need to plead the Blood of Jesus over our lives, so that the enemy can recognise that we live in the protection of the God Almighty.

I want to challenge you to think about any situation in your life right now where you sense very strongly the Holy Spirit is leading you to step away. Be bold and trust God, do not let money or the lack thereof place fear in your heart, no human or salary, nothing can provide for you the way that God can.

If you are in a relationship that you might fear actual physical harm if you choose to leave, I encourage you to seek God in prayer and ask the Holy Spirit to lead you to the right people to help you, you have God's angels with you, believe that and live according to that knowledge, no human can protect us like the God of Heaven and earth can.

MEDITATE

Psalms 119:114	You are my refuge and my shield; I have put my hope in your word.
Psalm 34:7-9	The angel of the LORD encamps around those who fear him, and he delivers them. Taste and see that the LORD is good; blessed is the one who takes refuge in him. Fear the LORD, you his holy people, for those who fear him lack nothing.
Isaiah 54:17	No weapon forged against you will prevail, and you will refute every tongue that accuses you. This is the heritage of the servants of the LORD, and this is their vindication from me," declares the LORD.
Psalm 17:8-10	Keep me as the apple of your eye; hide me in the shadow of your wings from the wicked who are out to destroy me, from my mortal enemies who surround me. They close up their callous hearts, and their mouths speak with arrogance.
Deuteronomy 31:6	Be strong and courageous. Do not be afraid or terrified because of them, for the LORD your God goes with you; he will never leave you nor forsake you."
Isaiah 8:12-13	Do not call conspiracy, everything this people calls a conspiracy do not fear what they fear, and do not dread it. The Lord Almighty is the one you are to regard as holy, he is the one you are to fear, he is the one you are to dread.

MY REFLECTIONS ON GOD'S PROTECTION

Where are you spending your time?

Where do you go to hide?

Where do you go to hide?

CHAPTER 8

LOVE SAYS: *I Will Discipline*

Hebrews 12:5-8
And have you completely forgotten this word of encouragement that addresses you as a father addresses his son? It says, "My son, do not make light of the Lord's discipline, and do not lose heart when he rebukes you, because the Lord disciplines the one he loves, and he chastens everyone he accepts as his son. Endure hardship as discipline; God is treating you as his children. For what children are not disciplined by their father? If you are not disciplined–and everyone undergoes discipline–then you are not legitimate, not true sons and daughters at all.

This book is about the amazing unfailing and incomparable love of God as our Father. So why talk about discipline, you might ask. Because it is clear in God's word that He disciplines the one, He loves and if we are not disciplined, we are not true daughters of God.

This truth will become clearer and more real when you get the revelation that God's discipline is always done in love, it is always for our good, always for His glory, and it is never to hurt us.

I am sure most of us know the Bible story about Jonah. We can all do well to sit back and ask the Holy Spirit to give us greater revelation into the life and lessons from the story of Jonah. Here we see that God's discipline of Jonah has a lot to do with His love for the lost, for Jonah, the world and everyone in it.

One of the definitions of discipline is "using punishment to correct disobedience".

When it comes to God's discipline, I believe discipline is the consequence of disobedience that will most of the time feel like punishment.

As a child, my nature had always been to do the right thing so that I would stay out of trouble. I really disliked being disciplined, so I figured the best thing would be to avoid it by being obedient. That automatically translated into my relationship with God; I was very careful to at least try to obey God. So, imagine my surprise when at the age of 31, I found myself in a Jonah situation.

I was working as a financial manager and felt very proud of what I was able to achieve. It was about a year after I returned to work from maternity leave, when new management had taken over and things started to change drastically and understandably, people were on edge, and some were starting to do whatever it would take to stay relevant be seen.

During this period, I felt the Holy Spirit leading me to resign; I started applying for other jobs, got some amazing interviews, but never got any of the jobs. The conviction to resign was very strong, but as I did not have a new job, it just did not seem like I was hearing God right, I fasted and prayed and during this time, I felt that God placed writing a book very strongly on my heart. I knew that God was saying I must resign, and I had to write the book.

I remember going to work and typing my resignation letter, which I saved in a folder. I just did not have the faith to resign without having another job, even though I knew I heard God right, I was embarrassed to tell people that God was telling me to resign and write a book. I know now that the big thing was that I was also not fully convinced that I had anything of true value to say in the form of a book. As I was driving to work one morning, the name of Jonah kept coming up in my heart; I must admit I got a little scared again. I did not tell anyone, especially my mother, because I knew what she would say, so I ignored God's voice. A few weeks later, I was driving with a colleague to a worksite, and we were having an unrelated conversation. He turned to me in the car and said, "Samantha, you sound just like Jonah from the Bible". I went cold inside because this time, God's warning was audible; I could almost picture myself in the big open seas, being swallowed by a huge great white shark. Still, my fear of what people would say, and my lack of faith in God's ability to use what I have been through, was stronger than my fear of what would happen if I stayed disobedient.

It was not long after this conversation that I was pushed beyond my limits. After months of build-up, I ended up leaving a meeting in tears, embarrassed and disappointed in God that He would allow me to suffer this kind of embarrassment. I had to be taken home as I could not even drive myself. I ended up in the office of a psychologist. It was during my one session with him when I realised I could not go back, and if I had just been obedient, things would not have turned out that way. I went back to work and resigned. My last day was the same day I had in my

original resignation letter, the one that I saved.
I do know that God would not have wanted things to end the way that they did; hence, all the very clear instructions and the warnings, but what I also realised after everything was that if I had chosen, even after that incident to stay, I would have lost my sanity. Only when I looked back, I could see the love in God allowing things to happen the way they did.

I wish I could tell you that I resigned and wrote that book, and I am living by the streams of living water because of being obedient to the call of God. Unfortunately, it took five more years, two other jobs, thousands of rands wasted on study fees and a few more hard consequences because of my disobedience.

Things changed completely when I realised that my being disobedient was affecting the people I had been called to serve; I now know that it was so much more about you, who are reading this book. I do not know who missed this book five years ago. All I can pray is that God will forgive me, that He would have brought someone else along that person's path or that He might allow them to still read it and that they will discover the greatest love of all.

I had to learn some hard lessons and go through some very unnecessary pain of discipline just like the prophet Jonah; my prayer is that you will be able to learn from what we have had to walk through and be bold in your faith to always choose obedience.
I do want to share what I had learned through my many disciplined moments and through the life of Jonah.

Who Is Your Nineveh?

Are you currently on a boat to Tarshish when you know full well God has been calling you in another direction?
Do you realise that there are people who need you to be obedient because their salvation depends on it?

Jonah 1:2
Go to the great city of Nineveh and preach against it, because its wickedness has come up before me.

Even as I write this, my heart still aches for those people who had to wait five more years for me to step out and become who God has called me to be.

We all have a Nineveh that is out there, it can be one person, or it can be millions, it can be your child, or it can be nations. So just remember this, you do not know who God has called you to serve, all you have to know is that you have been called to serve someone, so make haste to serve them the best you can.

Consequences Get Grace Too!

Yes, we all must face the consequences of our disobedience and yes, it will be hard and require great faith for us to be overcomers when the sting of discipline can so easily make us feel unloved by God.

We praise God for the truth of His word, God is love and He disciplines the ones He loves! I hope this truth brings you as much comfort as it did to me. It was only when I became a mother that I truly understood how this could be true. I am sometimes required to discipline my kids and that is never nice, but it is always for their benefit, and never ever not for a split second during this time of discipline have I ever felt less love for them; instead, it is because of my love for them that I do it and it hurts my heart when I must do it. But the most beautiful thing is when they are brave enough to come and say sorry afterwards. I can only imagine how God felt when He heard Jonah's prayer from the belly of the fish.

Jonah 2
"In my distress I called to the LORD, and he answered me.
From deep in the realm of the dead I called for help,
and you listened to my cry. You hurled me into the depths,
into the very heart of the seas, and the currents swirled about me;
all your waves and breakers swept over me.
I said, 'I have been banished from your sight;
yet I will look again toward your holy temple.'
The engulfing waters threatened me,[b] *the deep surrounded me;*
seaweed was wrapped around my head.
To the roots of the mountains I sank down;
the earth beneath barred me in forever. But you, LORD my God,
brought my life up from the pit. "When my life was ebbing away,
I remembered you, LORD, and my prayer rose to you,
to your holy temple. "Those who cling to worthless idols
turn away from God's love for them. But I, with shouts of grateful praise,
will sacrifice to you. What I have vowed I will make good.
I will say, 'Salvation comes from the LORD. "And the LORD
commanded the fish, and it vomited Jonah onto dry land.

We are God's daughters, His very own, do not ever let the devil try to convince you that being disciplined by God because of your own disobedience means that God does not love you. Jump over the boat even if it is more comfortable than the storm you will face after jumping. No comfort is worth staying in disobedience to God Almighty; you have the grace of God that will keep you safe even in the storm!

Obedience Is Better Than Sacrifice!

It took me five more years and a few more stormy boat rides before I stepped fully into obedience. Do not be like me; instead, I urge you to step fully into what God has called you to do right now. When Jonah went to give the message to Nineveh, you know by now that a whole nation; including, the king repented and was saved.

Jonah 3

Jonah obeyed the word of the Lord and went to Nineveh. Now Nineveh was a very large city; it took three days to go through it. Jonah began by going a day's journey into the city, proclaiming, "Forty more days and Nineveh will be overthrown." The Ninevites believed God. A fast was proclaimed, and all of them, from the greatest to the least, put on sackcloth. When Jonah's warning reached the king of Nineveh, he rose from his throne, took off his royal robes, covered himself with sackcloth and sat down in the dust. This is the proclamation he issued in Nineveh. "By the decree of the king and his nobles. Do not let people or animals, herds or flocks, taste anything; do not let them eat or drink. But let people and animals be covered with sackcloth. Let everyone call urgently on God. Let them give up their evil ways and their violence. Who knows? God may yet relent and with compassion turn from his fierce anger so that we will not perish. "When God saw what they did and how they turned from their evil ways, he relented and did not bring on them the destruction he had threatened.

Do you see that what Jonah had gone through was as much about God's love for Jonah as it was about His love for Nineveh? We were created by God, in God and for God. Every step of obedience is part of God's greater plan.

I pray that you will see God's obedience as an act of great Love towards you because you are His, He will do whatever is needed to get you to live with Him for all eternity. Nothing that is done is for now; everything is for the greater purpose of an eternity with the one who is Love.

MEDITATE

Proverb 12:1	Whoever loves discipline loves knowledge, but whoever hates correction is stupid.
Proverbs 3:11-12	My son, do not despise the Lord's discipline, and do not resent his rebuke, because the Lord disciplines those he loves, as a father the son he delights in.
Job 5:17	Blessed is the one whom God corrects, so do not despise the discipline of the Almighty.
Hebrews 12:11	No discipline seems pleasant at the time, but painful. Later on, however, it produces a harvest of righteousness and peace for those who have been trained by it.
Proverbs 10:17	Whoever heeds discipline shows the way to life, but whoever ignores correction leads others astray.
Revelations 3:19	Those whom I love I rebuke and discipline. So be earnest and repent.

MY REFLECTIONS ON GOD'S HEALING

Are you being disobedient?

Who is your Nineveh?

What does God require of you?

CHAPTER 9

LOVE SAYS: *All Things Are Possible*

Matthew 19:26
And looking at them Jesus said to them, "With people this is impossible, but with God all things are possible."

All through the Bible, we see so much evidence of how God made the impossible possible. One thing I had always desired was for us to have a house that we could call our own; during my childhood and teenage years in Gauteng, we moved so many times I do not have a count of that. After moving to Cape Town in 2002, we moved another eight times. Sometimes it was in houses, sometimes in people's garages and once in a shelter for abused women and children and even once in a room in a bush where the toilet was under a tree. I will always remember my mom praying to God for a piece of land to call her own.

I had my own private prayers, as I knew in my heart I desired to get married; I was trusting God for a husband and children and a home. I was very mindful that getting that and enjoying it would be difficult if my mom were still not settled. I committed to seeking God earnestly

in prayer and I started to believe in God for the provision to buy my mother a house. In the natural, this was completely impossible, even though I did have a well-paying job, buying a house on just my salary and committing to a 20-year bond was just not realistic and did not seem possible,
I chose not to focus on what seemed impossible, I had faith, so I started to look for houses. I had shared with some colleagues that I was looking for a house to buy and one day, while on study leave, I got a call about a house that was for sale. I got the address and took a drive past the house but decided not to contact the attorneys on that day; I planned to attend to it when I got back to work in two weeks.

Upon my return to work, I enquired about the house. It was still available, so I made an appointment for a viewing. When I arrived and walked through the house, I could feel that this was the piece of land my mother had prayed for. The asking price was too high; I knew I would not get bond approval, but God had given me some good negotiation skills, and after I excused myself and went into the main bedroom to talk to God, I felt the Holy Spirit give me the purchase amount. I immediately put in the offer even though it was almost half of what they were asking. The attorneys were keen to get me to put the offer in writing but tried to convince me to make the offer a little higher and assured me that the amount they were suggesting would definitely be accepted by the children. I knew that increasing the amount by a little would not make a big difference to the bond payment and the bank would probably approve the bond. But, immediately, I felt the Holy Spirit's presence. I knew that I could not go with any other price; I had to fight against the voice that said, you run the risk of not getting the house. I prayed that God would keep my faith strong and put in the offer I felt the Holy Spirit gave me.

The next morning at 9 am I got a call from the attorneys that the offer was accepted. I was blown away by how quickly it happened. I approached the bank for a home loan. While I was waiting on feedback from the bank, I got a call from the valuator who went out to value the house; he asked me how I can get the house for that price; it is worth much more. I was given a 100% bond, and by the age of 27, against all human impossibilities, I was able to buy my mother a house.

I remember calling her and telling her about her house. At first, she was not keen on moving, because the house was about 150km from where she was living at the time. She also voiced her concern about having to live with her children; she did not feel old enough for that. Even though I told her that it was her house, and I was not planning on living there with her for long she was not convinced.

After the transfer went through, she came to help me clean the house before moving in. It was the first time she saw the house; I knew that she felt the same way I did, that it was her piece of land that she had prayed for, for so long. Within a week, she packed up and moved. She is now living in her beautiful house, in a town that God called her to, to establish a women's ministry she now leads.

Tears are streaming down my face as I remember the faithfulness of God, His love is the only love with which can confidently say all things are possible, if we will only have faith and believe in the Love who is God.

For each of us, our most impossible situation will look different. But the one thing that will always remain the same is that God's word says no matter how impossible it is for man, all things are possible for Him.

We need to stay close to His voice always and we should not move away from His instructions even a little. I do not know what would have happened had I increased the amount by even just R1; all I know is that when God says something, we need to believe that because He loves us so greatly, He will do for us what no man can do and when God orders it He pays for it!

We Are Partners With God

2 Kings 4:1-7
The wife of a man from the company of the prophets cried out to Elisha, "Your servant my husband is dead, and you know that he revered the Lord. But now his creditor is coming to take my two boys as his slaves." Elisha replied to her, "How can I help you? Tell me, what do you have in your house?" "Your servant has nothing there at all," she said, "except a small jar of olive oil. Elisha said, "Go around and ask all your neighbors for empty jars. Don't ask for just a few. 4
Then go inside and shut the door behind you and your sons. Pour oil into all the jars, and as each is filled, put it to one side. "She left him and shut the door behind her and her sons. They brought the jars to her and she kept pouring. 6 When all the jars were full, she said to her son, "Bring me another one. "But," he replied, "There is not a jar left." Then the oil stopped flowing. She went and told the man of God, and he said, "Go, sell the oil and pay your debts. You and your sons can live on what is left."

We need to remember that whatever we are believing of God, His word does promise that for Him all things are possible, but the word also shows us that there will be certain requirements from our side too. We are partners with God.

We Must Have Faith

When we look at the widow in 2 Kings, we find her in a very desperate place, she is asking for help, but in response, she is asked, what do you have, she proceeds to answer and get an instruction to do something that might seem weird in the natural, to go and collect empty jars, but she obeys even though she only has a little bit of oil. Faith says I will go where I cannot see. For me, faith said search for a house, I will make a way for you to purchase it.

We Must Do Whatever God Says

When the woman had all the oil, she started throwing the oil into the jars; it was this act that was required, as silly as it must have seemed to her at the time, had she not taken that step and done exactly as she was told to do, she would have not only missed the provision that saved their lives she would have missed a miracle from the Lord God. When I got the amount from God, I could not change the amount; I might have missed the miracle that God had performed.

We must trust that where our abilities end, God's ability starts

This is the act of a miracle when we move beyond what we are able to do in the natural, to what God is able to do in the supernatural. Because the woman poured the oil, but she could not make it more than it was, God steps in and does the impossible, and He supernaturally increases the oil supply. When I obeyed God and stuck to the price, I was given by the Holy Spirit, He supernaturally cut the asking price of the house in half.

Live with bold faith, dare to believe that the greatest Love of all has chosen you and will make the impossible possible for you, simply because He loves you!

God's love for you gives you access to the impossible here on earth, but it is your faith in God's love that will activate the impossible and allow you to receive and enjoy a life overflowing with impossible moments. Dear God, I pray the word of faith will take root in the heart of everyone reading this book; I pray that every Scripture will be activated as they meditate on your word and believe in the power of the Blood of Jesus and the Holy Spirit that is living inside of them.

MEDITATE

Philippians 4:13	I can do all this through him who gives me strength.
Luke 1:37	For no word from God will ever fail.
Mark 9:23	"'If you can'?" said Jesus. "Everything is possible for one who believes."
Matthew 17:20	He replied, "Because you have so little faith. Truly I tell you, if you have faith as small as a mustard seed, you can say to this mountain, 'Move from here to there,' and it will move. Nothing will be impossible for you."
Job 42:2	"I know that you can do all things, no purpose of yours can be thwarted."
Jeremiah 32:17	"Ah, Sovereign Lord, you have made the heavens and the earth by your great power and outstretched arm. Nothing is too hard for you."

MY REFLECTIONS ON THE IMPOSSIBLE

Do you have faith?

What does God require of you?

CHAPTER 10

LOVE SAYS: *You Are Empowered*

Proverb 31:10-31
A wife of noble character who can find?
She is worth far more than rubies. Her husband has full confidence in her
and lacks nothing of value. She brings him good, not harm,
all the days of her life. She selects wool and flax
and works with eager hands. She is like the merchant ships,
bringing her food from afar. She gets up while it is still night;
she provides food for her family and portions for her female servants.
She considers a field and buys it; out of her earnings she plants a
vineyard. She sets about her work vigorously;
her arms are strong for her tasks. She sees that her trading is profitable,
and her lamp does not go out at night. In her hand she holds the distaff
and grasps the spindle with her fingers. She opens her arms to the poor
and extends her hands to the needy. When it snows, she has no fear for her household;
for all of them are clothed in scarlet. She makes coverings for her bed;
she is clothed in fine linen and purple. Her husband is respected at the city gate,
where he takes his seat among the elders of the land. She makes linen garments and sells them,
and supplies the merchants with sashes. She is clothed with strength and dignity;
she can laugh at the days to come. She speaks with wisdom,
and faithful instruction is on her tongue. She watches over the affairs of her household
and does not eat the bread of idleness. Her children arise and call her blessed;

her husband also, and he praises her. "Many women do noble things, but you surpass them all." Charm is deceptive, and beauty is fleeting; but a woman who fears the Lord is to be praised. Honor her for all that her hands have done, and let her works bring her praise at the city gate.

I think that when we think of a powerful woman, we can be very one dimensional in our thinking. We immediately might think, businesswomen, politicians, doctors, lawyers, sports stars, movie stars, and influencers. Yes, you are right; all those accolades will make someone powerful or feel powerful.

As I am writing this book, we are in the middle of the worst pandemic the world has ever seen, which has caused us to go into an unprecedented lockdown and isolation. A few months ago I felt God lead me in a different direction; I felt the call to homeschool my children. So, at the beginning of 2021, I stepped into the role of full-time mom, homemaker, and home-schooler.

As I settled into this new role, I was surprised by the overwhelming sense of worthlessness I felt on many days. The reason I was so surprised was because I did expect to feel some sense of loss and had tried to mentally prepare myself for those moments by talking to my husband about it often. But the feeling was not just a sense of feeling I had lost my worth or ability to bring some financial support; it was so much deeper than that.

When you are in the corporate world, and you get to the point in your life where people start to recognise you as an expert in your field, that is the kind of validation that we live for, right? For many of us, the positions we hold are what give us that sense of accomplishment and feeling of

power.
I felt that, having held positions as financial manager and business consultant, people respected me, I had the opportunity to be a leader. And suddenly, the thing I was now known for was being a mother and a homemaker. I did not feel any sense of being powerful, and you know, as Christian women, we all strive to be like the proverbs 31 women. The perfect homemaker, the perfect businesswoman, the perfect boss, the perfect wife, and so the list goes on and on.

From Sacrificed To Privileged

When I started on this journey of full-time mom and teacher, my sweet 5-year-old son was such an introvert. He was naturally shy and quiet. At first, it did not concern me as my husband is an introvert, so I just assumed that it was an inherent trait from his father. But because I was now more present, I started to realise that he became easily overwhelmed with people and did not do well with people putting pressure on him to do things. He did not do well with making new friends, even to the point that if new children arrived on the playground, he would stop playing and chose to sit with me and if I pushed too hard for him to go play, he would burst into tears. As a mother, this broke my heart.

But because I knew there was a real problem, I started to pray about it, and I worked hard on the way I approached his schoolwork and his interaction with other kids. With my focus being on him, at first, I did not realise that I was feeling less of my own worthless feelings. Slowly I started to see him change and confidence in him beginning to show. One specific day a few months ago, I remember him running into the house and asking me if he could go play with a boy he had not seen for a long time; as I watched my once shy, introverted son play confidently and completely happy, I remember a bittersweet feeling come over me. I did that! Me being there, being present, me praying specifically was what had changed things for my son. And in a split second, the word sacrifice (because many days I felt like I sacrificed my career) became the word privilege. No, I did not sacrifice my career; I had the privilege to be a full-time homeschooling mom.

You are called to be powerful!

My Perspective changed on that day, but the greater revelation was still to come.

Proverbs 31:17
She sets about her work vigorously, her arms are strong for her tasks.

As I go back to the book of Proverbs and read about this phenomenal woman God has given all of us the ability to be, I realised that being powerful is not connected to our accolades or titles or how many of these roles we can hold at once and manage perfectly.

The revelation that God gave me is that He has given us the ability to be powerful and that power lies in how well we serve where we have been called to serve. Each of us has been called to something very specific and that might change from season to season. But the one thing that always remains the same is whatever the role is, it is always in service of others, and if we set out about what we have been called to vigorously, our arms will be strong for our task.

In this season of my life, I am standing in service of a 4-and 6-year-old, and I have chosen to serve them the best God have equipped me to do; I will serve them as well as I would have served a nation should I have been the president of a country, because this is what I have been called to do right now, and I am the best, most equipped person to do this only because God has chosen me and I will continue to seek God and listen to His voice. I want to impact their lives with a heart of service and trust that this will equip them to impact the lives that they have been called to serve.

God loves us; He empowers us to become all He has created us to be. All we need to do is be obedient to the call.

As women, we have been called to be powerful; God, who created us, has so much confidence in us. If we can only believe the same for our own lives. We do not have to compare our lives to other women; we need to stay in our lane and serve well where God has called us to serve. The power of God's anointing rests in that place. When we step into our true calling, we will, without a doubt, change the world.

The Bible proves that we stand alongside the superwomen who have gone before us and today, we take courage from their act of serving boldly in the place they have been called to serve.

We were chosen to birth the Saviour of the world.
Meet Mary, the mother of Jesus.
We were chosen to save a nation from the wrath of a king.
Meet Queen Ester.
We were chosen to destroy an army and lead with compassion.
Meet Deborah, the prophetess.

We were chosen to save the baby Moses, who would lead the Israelites out of Egypt. Meet Miriam, the sister of Moses.
We were chosen to stop powerful King David, a man after God's own heart, from committing murder. Meet Abigail, the wife of Nabal.

We are powerful beyond measure; how we use that power matters. I want to encourage you to find your power. Seek God; we have all been called to something greater than ourselves. Woman, you hold within yourself the ability to change a life, that can change a city, that can change a nation, that can change the world. Be brave, be powerful and be who God called you to be.

MEDITATE

Psalms 46:5	God is within her, she will not fall, God will help her at break of day.
1 Corinthians 15:10	But by the grace of God I am what I am, and his grace to me was not without effect. No, I worked harder than all of them–yet not I, but the grace of God that was with me.
1 Corinthians 11:11	Nevertheless, in the Lord woman is not independent of man, nor is man independent of woman.
Luke 1:45	Blessed is she who has believed that the Lord would fulfill his promises to her!"
Joshua 1:9	Have I not commanded you? Be strong and courageous. Do not be afraid; do not be discouraged, for the Lord your God will be with you wherever you go."
Luke 10:19	I have given you authority to trample on snakes and scorpions and to overcome all the power of the enemy; nothing will harm you.
2 Peter 1:3	His divine power has given us everything we need for a godly life through our knowledge of him who called us by his own glory and goodness.

MY REFLECTIONS ON BEING EMPOWERED

What have you struggled with?

What does being empowered look like for you?

CHAPTER 11

LOVE SAYS: *You Are Enough*

Genesis 1:27
So God created mankind in His Own Image, in the image of God He created them, male and female He created them.

Let me just say this," You are Beautiful, you are Worthy, you are Enough!!

Do not be surprised when I tell you that I struggled to truly believe this for a very long time. Being created in God's image should be enough reason to believe that you are beautiful, worthy, and enough, right? For the longest time in my life, being a born-again believer, I tried to convince myself and other people to believe all those things about myself.

Believing that God loved me means I needed to believe in the fullness of what Him loving me means, but I did not understand God's love completely. When I look back on my life, I was a great pretender. Because I convinced myself I believed it, it was easy for me to pretend publicly while in private I had a war in my heart as I never did feel good enough or beautiful. In my 27th year of life, I realised that pretence will only ever get me to a certain point. Then I needed to face the hard truths that I had been living a lie, and I had been struggling with low self-esteem for years.

In high school, I attended a predominantly white school; being a girl of colour in that environment had its own challenges. I started to develop insecurities about my hair texture, my voice had always been deep, I had bad acne during my teenage years, and because of the environment I was in, boys were not really interested in me; this added to me not feeling beautiful at all. But as a Christian and as someone who was very verbal about my relationship and love for Jesus Christ, I was able to cover that up, because after all, it was a sin to believe that God created me ugly and that I was not good enough.

Yet, there were times when those feelings would come to the surface, and they always came in the worst ways. But I remember that when I was 17 years old, God stretches forth His hand of deliverance in love, the love that says you are enough, beautifully created in my image.

The one thing that I did have as a teenager was good friends at youth, and I was the “friend” to the boys. You know, the one everyone would confide in about who they were crushing on, but never the one anyone ever crushed on. One night during a church service, I was sitting next to some friends when God’s call of deliverance was extended to me.

We had an international preacher giving the word, who spoke directly to me, describing every feeling of insecurity, every act of pretence I have maintained over the years; there was no confusion in my heart that God was speaking to me, the preacher might as well have said my name. I remember my heart was racing. I was so scared, I kept thinking that if I got up, everyone would know the truth about what I really think of myself, and my secret would be out. I could not bring myself to get up.

After the service, I attempted to rectify my disobedience in private by going to the preacher and admitting that I was the girl he was talking about and that I needed deliverance from low self-esteem. His response to me that night would haunt me for 10 years; he said that the moment had passed, that the anointing healing power of God had rested at the moment he spoke to me in the service.

I know for some of you that might not sound very loving, and as a 17-year-old girl, I certainly could not see the love or grace at that moment as I did not completely understand the supernatural workings of God. But I know now that the Holy Spirit comes, and an invitation will be given to you, and if you do not react to that moment, the anointing will lift. And it might just take ten more years of suffering, scarred relationships, joy incomplete, where in an instant, that feeling of not being enough would overwhelm you to the point of complete despair.

I was 27 years old, and by this time, I had achieved so much and even competed in modelling competitions, when I had one of those moments again. This time it would be my mother's words that would get me to reflect more on why this was happening to me. I remember her asking me, 'you love God so much, and you believe everything about Him. Why are you struggling so much with believing that you are beautiful and enough?" Those words struck me, and I was overcome by emotions; I was overwhelmed by the question. Lord, I love you, you love me, you have given me so much and proved your love to me; why am I not able to believe this one thing about myself, that I am enough! I knew what the Bible said in Psalm 139:14 "I praise you because I am fearfully and wonderfully made, your works are wonderful, I know that full well", but my head and my heart would not align with this knowledge.

I started to really press in to God and seek Him for deliverance, not forgetting the words from the preacher 10 years before; I had to hold onto the hope that God was a gracious God and that He would create another opportunity for my healing.

And true to His nature, my God did provide another opportunity, and again, it was in front of a crowd of people, but this time I did not run from the call; I did not allow my fear of people opinions to rob me of living free and in victory over low-self-esteem. As the Holy Spirit convicted me of repenting and sharing my testimony, I was obedient and started by sharing my story of 10 years ago. As I spoke, and the tears came down my face, and as I confessed my sins of disobedience, I felt the healing power of deliverance wash over me. That was the day I believed for the very first time that my outward appearance was created by God fearfully and wonderfully, and I am beautiful and that I am enough. That was the day I finally realised that no makeup, clothes, or how many titles I add to my achievements, those things do not and will never define me as being enough; I am enough because God loves me.

This revelation changed the way I speak, the way I present myself to people. Many times, the enemy will still want to come and whisper the lies of unworthiness, but then I am reminded of the love of God that says, I love you, you are worth me sending my Son to die for you, you are enough.

God has been so faithful in keeping my heart in check in this area. It was just over a year ago when one day God spoke to me about the dependence that I had started placing on makeup again. He was very clear in saying that He doesn't have an issue with me wearing makeup, but He was always concerned about the reason why I was wearing it, and at that moment, I realised that I have made a small idol and sifted my focus off the word of God concerning what feel about myself.

What I have learned is that I must renew my mind daily in this *area (Romans 12:2 - Do not conform any longer to the pattern of this world, but be transformed by the renewing of your mind...),* you see the enemy will always seek to have us fall in those areas where we have seen the victory.

So now, on a daily basis, I must do as the Bible says in *2 Corinthians 10:5 - We demolish arguments and every pretension that sets itself up against the knowledge of God, and we take captive every thought to make it obedient to Christ.*

True Confidence Comes In Knowing You Are Enough

Ruth 2:2-8

And Ruth the Moabitess said to Naomi, "Let me go to the fields and pick up the leftover grain behind anyone in whose eyes I find favor." Naomi said to her, "Go ahead, my daughter." So she went out and began to glean in the fields behind the harvesters. As it turned out, she found herself working in a field belonging to Boaz, who was from the clan of Elimelech. Just then Boaz arrived from Bethlehem and greeted the harvesters, "The LORD be with you!" "The LORD bless you!" they called back. Boaz asked the foreman of his harvesters, "Whose young woman is that?" The foreman replied, "She is the Moabitess who came back from Moab with Naomi. She said, `Please let me glean and gather among the sheaves behind the harvesters.' She went into the field and has worked steadily from morning till now, except for a short rest in the shelter. "So Boaz said to Ruth, "My daughter, listen to me. Don't go and glean in another field and don't go away from here. Stay here with my servant girls.

When we look at the life of Ruth. We are introduced to a young widow who was so committed to loving well that she was unwilling to let her mother-in-law Naomi go off alone. Ruth left her whole family and her homeland to follow Naomi to a land and a people she did not know.

We see that when Ruth and Naomi arrived, she did not just sit around or try to find a husband; the first thing she did was go into the field to work, so she was able to provide for herself and her mother-in-law. What stood out to me most about Ruth was her strong, confident character. Ruth certainly was not looking to find her worth in things or people; she was simply living in love and keeping busy by working in the fields.

She was the one who suggested to Naomi that she wanted to go into the fields, she was the one who went into the fields and asked the overseer if she could gather amongst the sheaves, and she was the one who worked hard and got noticed. This all speaks of a confident woman.

In all her confidence, she remained humble. Ruth was a beautiful woman. I mean, Boas immediately noticed her. But she humbly asked him why she deserves his favour. And we see that Ruth's reputation preceded her. I believe that a good reputation will always follow a life that is lived in the fullness of who God called you to be.

One of the most common things the enemy will get us to do when we do not know our value in who Jesus Christ says we are is to convince us that what we do, what we say and how we act does not matter. I want to tell you today that it always matters.

We never know who we are meant to meet in our lifetime. We might not even know who we have truly been called to be. And one day, when those people and truths are revealed, what type of reputation will we have built.

Ruth is part of the Bloodline of Jesus Christ, the saviour of the world. I do not think that when Ruth lost her first husband, and she basically chose to lay down her own life (by leaving her family, her country, her gods) for a life with her mother-in-law, did she for one moment think that a purpose so great awaits her. All she did was know her worth, she loved well, and she chose God.

You are God's Masterpiece!

Ephesians 2:10
For we are God's handiwork, created in Christ Jesus to do good works, which God prepared in advanced for us to do.

I want to encourage today to make a choice now to believe God's word. You have been called by God, chosen by God and you are loved by God. Being beautiful does not qualify you, being smart does not qualify you, being rich does not qualify you, being successful does not qualify you, none of these things qualifies you as being enough, yet believing what God says about you qualifies you and that will lead to all of the above!

Know your worth, love yourself, love people and always choose God. You might not yet know who you have been called to serve or who you have been called to be but know this for sure that you have been called for signs, wonder and miracles and who God created you to be enough!! Believe that!!!

MEDITATE

Proverbs 3:15	She is more precious than rubies, nothing you desire can compare with her.
1 Peter 3:3-4	Your beauty should not come from outward adornment, such as elaborate hairstyles and the wearing of gold jewellery or fine clothes. Rather, it should be that of your inner self, the unfading beauty of a gentle and quiet spirit, which is of great worth in God's sight.
1 John 3:1	See what great love the Father has lavished on us, that we should be called children of God! And that is what we are! The reason the world does not know us is that it did not know him.
1 Timothy 3:11	In the same way, the women[a] are to be worthy of respect, not malicious talkers but temperate and trustworthy in everything.
1 Peter 2:9	But you are a chosen people, a royal priesthood, a holy nation, God's special possession, that you may declare the praises of him who called you out of darkness into his wonderful light.

MY REFLECTIONS ON BEING ENOUGH

What are you struggling to believe about yourself?

What does God say about you?

CHAPTER 12

LOVE SAYS: *You Are Mine*

Romans 8: 38-39
For I am convinced that neither death nor life, neither angels nor demons, neither the present nor the future, nor any powers, neither height nor depth, nor anything else in all creation, will be able to separate us from the love of God that is in Christ Jesus our Lord.

When I first discovered the truth that I belong to God, it was the most exciting revelation; being a teenager at the time wanting to just know that someone, anyone really, would just say you are mine is something we all crave.

At thirteen, I was a very eager Christian. I was fascinated by this idea that God loved us so much that He gave His only Beloved Son to die for us on the cross. Every morning before school, I would pray and read my Bible. My weekends were filled with youth and church services, and during the week, I would attend Bible study sessions with our youth group. The more I learned about who God was, the more I wanted to know. God's love was very real to me from the start, and I wanted nothing more than to believe everything the Bible said about God. To me, He became a Father in every way and I truly felt like I belonged to the family of Jesus Christ.

As I grew older, I would often hear the testimonies of young women telling their stories of how the rejection they received from the earthly father caused them not to trust men. They would seek love and acceptance in all the wrong places, which led them further into shame and rejection. Many of these stories were like my story, and even though I had to fight through many struggles, it never got to the point that I was willing to settle for anything less than what I believed God promised for me. I wondered a lot about this over the years.

One specific night I was 29 years old and engaged to be married by this time. I attended a connect group where a young man told his story of how bitter he was and how hard he struggled with his relationship with God because of his broken relationship with his biological father. It took him years to separate who God was from who his earthly father was; it was only when he was able to do that, that he was able to truly accept God as Lord and Father of his life.

After that Bible study session I remember asking God why it seemed easier for me to just accept His love, why even in all my struggles, I was always able to come back to the knowledge that His love was the standard for me. That night God spoke into my heart. He said because you accepted me not only as God but as your Father, you gave me the great privilege of being what I am to everyone who accepts the gift of fatherhood that I freely give. The Bible teaches us that we have been called to be co-heirs with Jesus Christ; the truth of this is that we are not merely visitors or servants in the house of God; we are His very own. It is in believing, truly accepting, and, most importantly, living this truth to discover the beauty of having God as our Father.

As a mother, I now understand this even more. I look at my two beautiful children God entrusted into my life for me to take care of and lead and guide through this life. I love them so much; they are mine, everything I have belongs to them. My greatest desire is to always give them a safe place to live in this world. As a mother, I know that there is nothing I would not do for them, and when I look at them with their childlike faith, they believe that they belong to me, when they need anything, they come to me, they simply believe that they are mine and know that it means everything I have is theirs.

I might one day disappoint them in my human capacity, but with God, our Father, we never have to fear that He will ever disappoint us; every promise He makes will stand firm because He is the promise keeper.

What an amazing, life-changing realisation! We belong to God. He is our Father; everything He has belongs to us; nothing that we have done and nothing that we can do will ever be able to separate us from the love of God Almighty.

If you are like the young man standing in the brokenness and rejection of your earthly father, I want to tell you today that where you come from and who has been chosen to be your biological parents will never define you; it will not determine who you have been called to be only God who created you decides who you will be. God is not our parent; He does not possess the ability to ever disappoint us; the love He has for us is pure, unconditional, and eternal. Do not compare the love of God to the love of people.

This is what I want to share with you today, beautiful princess, daughter of the Most High King. My life changed at the young age of thirteen years old because I dared to believe that the God of the universe loves me, that He calls me His own. This truth has saved me completely, and I will forever seek to praise His holy name.

To this world, we might be seen as fatherless, as poor, as untalented, as ugly, but I want to tell you that God is your Father, He is your creator, you are the great love of His life, you are the daughter of the King of kings and can take your rightful place in the presence of our Father, you belong to the family of Jesus Christ.

You have been called for a time such as this. God loves you. He gave His only Son for you, and even if you were the only person on this earth, Jesus Christ would still have died on the cross for you.

Today is the day that God is calling your name; He is reaching out to you with His arms wide open. You need to know that your brokenness, sin, disappointments, and the life you have lived until today are your past. God is standing ready to give you a new life; He is ready to lead you as Father and King. You have been called to live in the fullness of who He says you are; you have been called to be loved completely, with a love that has no limitation and no conditions.

My prayer is that you will accept the love of God, accept Jesus Christ as your personal Lord and Saviour and that you will step into the call God has on your life and live a life filled with the power of the Holy Spirit. May you experience everything that the love of God is. You have been made in love, by love and for love.
Live loved and love well!

Today I am asking you again to put your trust in Jesus Christ and pray this prayer.
Prayer of Salvation!

PRAYER OF SALVATION

Dear heavenly Father, I know that I am a sinner, and I ask for Your forgiveness. I believe Jesus died for my sins and rose from the dead. I turn from my sins, I repent of my sins, and I invite You to come into my heart and life. I want to trust and follow You as my Lord and Saviour. In the Mighty Name of Jesus. Amen

---

This Love Is Forever!

Psalm 136
Give thanks to the Lord, for he is good.
His love endures forever. Give thanks to the God of gods.
His love endures forever. Give thanks to the Lord of lords:
His love endures forever, to him who alone does great wonders,
His love endures forever, who by his understanding made the heavens,
His love endures forever, who spread out the earth upon the waters,
His love endures forever, who made the great lights—
His love endures forever, the sun to govern the day,
His love endures forever, the moon and stars to govern the night;
His love endures forever, to him who struck down the firstborn of Egypt
His love endures forever and brought Israel out from among them
His love endures forever, with a mighty hand and outstretched arm;
His love endures forever, to him who divided the Red Sea[a] asunder
His love endures forever, and brought Israel through the midst of it,
His love endures forever, but swept Pharaoh and his army into the Red Sea;
His love endures forever, to him who led his people through the wilderness;
His love endures forever, to him who struck down great kings,
His love endures forever, and killed mighty kings—
His love endures forever, Sihon king of the Amorites
His love endures forever, and Og king of Bashan—
His love endures forever, and gave their land as an inheritance,
His love endures forever, an inheritance to his servant Israel.
His love endures forever, He remembered us in our low estate
His love endures forever, and freed us from our enemies.
His love endures forever, He gives food to every creature.
His love endures forever, Give thanks to the God of heaven.
His love endures forever

www.ingramcontent.com/pod-product-compliance
Lightning Source LLC
Chambersburg PA
CBHW031626040426
42452CB00007B/689
9781776306817